Small Coverlet
Instructions on page 2.

Small Coverlet, *shown on page 1.*

MATERIALS:

Cream sheeting, 90 cm by 250 cm. Floral prints: Pink and cream, 90 cm by 65 cm each; blue and beige, 80 cm by 65 cm each. Olive green gingham checks, 15 cm square. Quilt batting, 85.5 cm by 112 cm. White cotton lace edging, 3 cm by 60 cm. Iron-on interfacing, 25 cm square. Polyester fiberfill.

FINISHED SIZE: 85.5 cm by 112 cm.

Appliqué Pattern   Add 0.7 cm all around for seam allowance.

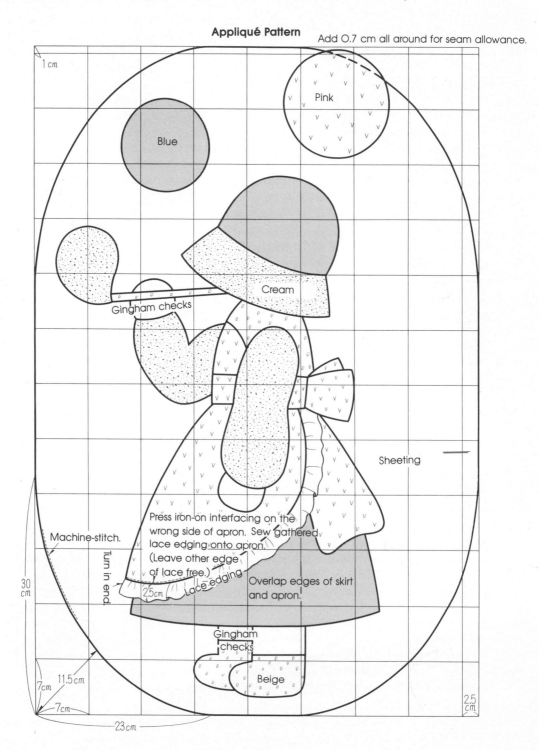

1 cm

Pink

Blue

Cream

Gingham checks

Sheeting

Machine-stitch.

Press iron-on interfacing on the wrong side of apron. Sew gathered lace edging onto apron. (Leave other edge of lace free.)

Turn in end.

2.5 cm

Lace edging

Overlap edges of skirt and apron.

Gingham checks

Beige

30 cm

11.5 cm

7 cm

7 cm

23 cm

2.5 cm

DIRECTIONS:

① Sew pieces for top together.

② Place lining, batting and pieced top together and quilt on the seams by machine.

③ Bind edges with cream sheeting.

④ Sew oval sheeting piece onto top by machine.

⑤ Turn in seam allowance of appliqué pieces and slip-stitch onto oval sheeting, catching background fabric. Stuff thinly with fiberfill as you appliqué.

Piecing Diagram

Add 1 cm all around for seam allowance.

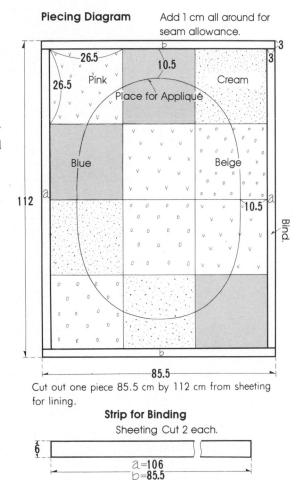

Cut out one piece 85.5 cm by 112 cm from sheeting for lining.

Strip for Binding

Sheeting Cut 2 each.

6
a=106
b=85.5

Pink Mat, *shown on page 5.*

MATERIALS:

Cotton broadcloth: White with pink flowers, 87 cm by 6 cm; pink with white flowers and fabric for lining, 20 cm in diameter each. Quilt batting, 20 cm in diameter. White cotton lace edging, 2 cm by 87 cm.

FINISHED SIZE: 26 cm in diameter.

DIRECTIONS:

① Place lining, batting and pink top together and quilt horizontally and vertically to make 3 cm square grid by machine.

② Fold long edge of ruffle twice and machine-stitch. Sew ends together to form circle.

③ Sew ends of lace to form circle and place on ruffle. Run gathering stitches on both ruffle and lace. Place quilted circle on gathered lace and ruffle and top-stitch.

Diagram

Add 1 cm all around for seam allowance.

Zigzag stitch along raw edges.

Mat

Pink with white flowers   Cut 1.

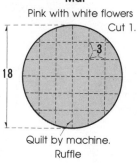

18

3

Quilt by machine.

Ruffle

White with pink flowers   Cut 1.

4

85

Finished Diagram

Sew ends of ruffle and lace individually, gather both and sew on quilted circle.

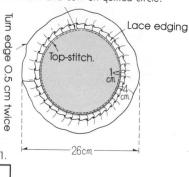

Turn edge 0.5 cm twice and machine-stitch.

Top-stitch.

Lace edging

1 cm

4 cm

26cm

3

Glasses Case, Cosmetic Case, Pencil Case, Tissue Cases and Mat
Instructions for Glasses Case and Cosmetic Case on page 6, for Pencil Case and
Tissue Case on page 83 and for Mat on page 3.

Glasses Case and Cosmetic Case, *shown on* page 4.

Glasses Case

MATERIALS:

Cotton broadcloth: Yellow with white flowers, 40 cm square; white with yellow flowers, 18 cm by 20 cm; green with white dots, 7 cm by 5 cm. Bright yellow sheeting, 7 cm by 10 cm. Six-strand embroidery floss No. 25 in brown. Quilt batting, 18 cm by 20 cm. Velcro, 2.5 cm by 1.5 cm. Polyester fiberfill.

FINISHED SIZE: See diagram.

DIRECTIONS:

① Cut out pieces adding no seam allowance except top edge. Place lining, batting and top together and baste. Quilt along 3 cm-square grid lines.

② Embroider on sheeting in chain and cross stitches. Make up for glasses case, following instructions from step 1 to 4 shown in finished diagram.

Cutting Diagram

Zigzag-stitch along raw edges by machine.

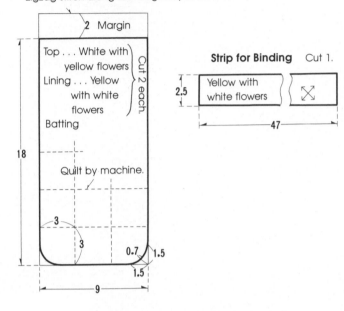

Strip for Binding   Cut 1.

Appliqué Pattern (Actual Size)

Add 0.5 cm all around for seam allowance.

Finished Diagram

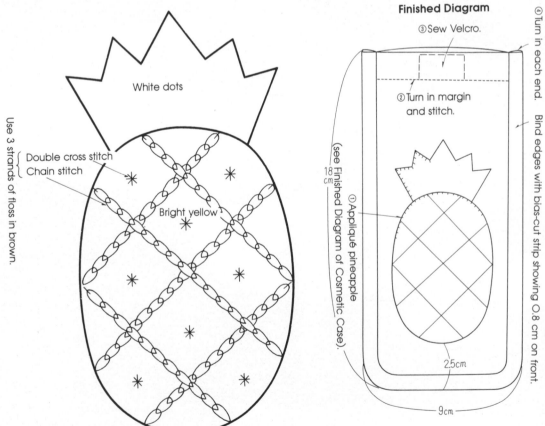

Cosmetic Case

MATERIALS:

Cotton broadcloth: Yellow with white flowers, 40 cm square; white with yellow flowers, 24 cm by 17 cm; green with white dots, 8 cm by 6 cm. Bright yellow sheeting, 8 cm by 10 cm. Six-strand embroidery floss No. 25 in brown. Quilt batting, 24 cm by 17 cm. Polyester fiberfill. 10 cm-long zipper.

FINISHED SIZE: See diagram.

DIRECTIONS:

① Cut out pieces adding no seam allowance. Place lining, batting and top together and baste. Quilt along 3 cm-square grid lines.

② Embroider on sheeting in chain and double cross stitches. Make up for Cosmetic Case, following steps 1 to 4 shown in finished diagram.

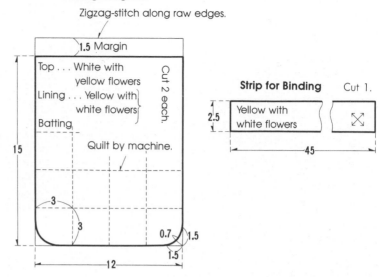

Cutting Diagram

Zigzag-stitch along raw edges.

1.5 Margin

Top . . . White with yellow flowers
Lining . . . Yellow with white flowers
Batting

Cut 2 each.

Quilt by machine.

15

3

3

0.7   1.5

1.5

12

Strip for Binding   Cut 1.

2.5   Yellow with white flowers

45

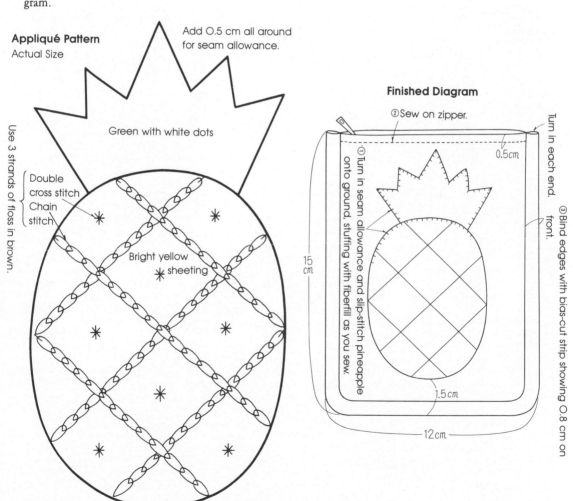

Appliqué Pattern
Actual Size

Add 0.5 cm all around for seam allowance.

Green with white dots

Use 3 strands of floss in brown.

Double cross stitch
Chain stitch

Bright yellow sheeting

Finished Diagram

② Sew on zipper.

0.5 cm

Turn in each end.

① Turn in seam allowance and slip-stitch pineapple onto ground, stuffing with fiberfill as you sew.

③ Bind edges with bias-cut strip showing 0.8 cm on front.

15 cm

1.5 cm

12 cm

7

Pillows

Instructions on page 10.

MATERIALS:

Even-weave cotton fabric: For Pillow at left: Rose pink with pink dots, 90 cm by 40 cm; pink with floral designs, 90 cm by 30 cm; coral pink, 25 cm square; soft pink with small flowers, 35 cm by 7 cm; gray, 45 cm by 5 cm; beige, 10 cm square; wine red, 17 cm by 11 cm; brown, 6 cm square. Sewing thread in brown, gray and

Cutting Diagram

Add 1cm all around for seam allowance unless otherwise indicated.

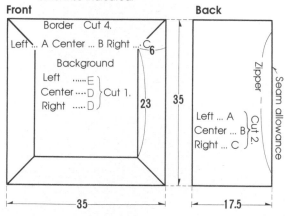

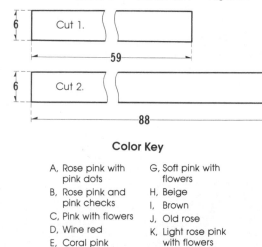

Color Key

A, Rose pink with pink dots	G, Soft pink with flowers
B, Rose pink and pink checks	H, Beige
C, Pink with flowers	I, Brown
D, Wine red	J, Old rose
E, Coral pink	K, Light rose pink with flowers
F, Gray	

colors matching the appliqués. For Pillow at center: Rose pink and pink checks, 90 cm by 45 cm; rose pink with pink dots, 90 cm by 30 cm; wine red, 25 cm square; light pink with flowers, 90 cm by 7 cm; old rose, 45 cm by 7 cm; gray, 45 cm by 5 cm; soft pink with flowers, 21 cm by 7 cm. Sewing thread in colors matching the appliqués. For Pillow at right: Pink with floral design, 90 cm by 40 cm; rose pink and pink checks, 90 cm by 24 cm; wine red, 40 cm by 25 cm; soft pink with flowers, 56 cm by 7 cm; gray, 45 cm by 5 cm; beige, 15 cm by 6 cm; brown, 6 cm square. Sewing thread in brown and colors matching the appliqués. For each pillow: 30 cm-long zipper. Inner pillow stuffed with kapok, 35 cm square. FINISHED SIZE: See diagram.

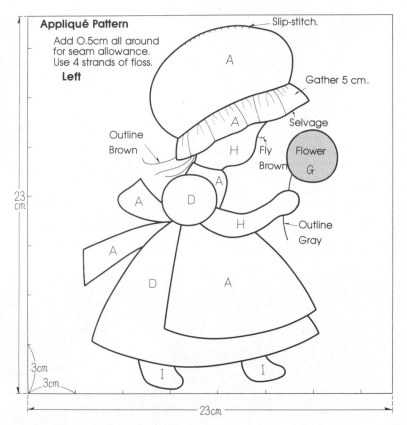

DIRECTIONS:

① Cut out pieces adding 1cm all around for seam allowance except center back edges and appliqué pieces. Enlarge appliqué pattern as indicated and cut out pieces adding 0.5cm all around for seam allowance.

Appliqué
(Actual Size)
Add 0.5cm for seam allowance.

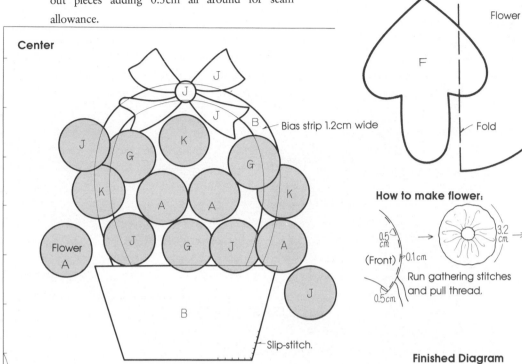

Center

Bias strip 1.2cm wide

Flower A

Slip-stitch.

3cm
3cm

Flower F

Flower

Fold

How to make flower:

0.5 cm
(Front) 0.1cm
0.5cm

Run gathering stitches and pull thread.

3.2 cm

Place flower on background and take 5 - 6 stitches.

Finished Diagram

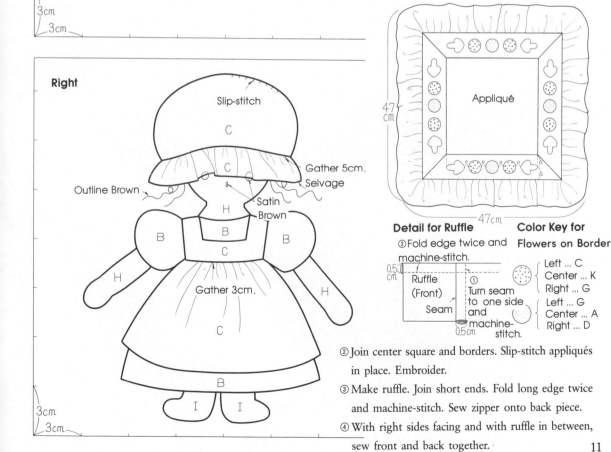

Right

Slip-stitch

Outline Brown

Gather 5cm.
Selvage

Satin Brown

Gather 3cm.

3cm
3cm

Appliqué

47 cm

47cm

Detail for Ruffle

② Fold edge twice and machine-stitch.

0.5 cm
Ruffle (Front)
Seam
① Turn seam to one side and machine-stitch.
0.5cm

Color Key for Flowers on Border

Left ... C
Center ... K
Right ... G

Left ... G
Center ... A
Right ... D

② Join center square and borders. Slip-stitch appliqués in place. Embroider.

③ Make ruffle. Join short ends. Fold long edge twice and machine-stitch. Sew zipper onto back piece.

④ With right sides facing and with ruffle in between, sew front and back together.

11

Pincushions and Scissors Cases
Instructions for Pincushions on page 14 and for
Scissors Cases on page 86.

Pincushions, shown on page 12.

MATERIALS:

For A: Dull mauve sheeting, 26cm by 10cm. Cotton broadcloth, pink with flowers, 10cm by 6cm. White sewing thread, #50. For B: Cotton broadcloth: White with lavender flowers, 20cm by 10cm; lavender and peony rose, 12cm by 6cm each. White sewing thread, #50. For C: Purple velveteen, 24cm by 12cm. Cotton broadcloth with floral designs in sky blue, pink, lavender and blue, 5cm square each. White lace edging, 1cm by 35cm. For D: Blue-gray sheeting, 27cm by 10cm. Cotton broadcloth: Navy with white flowers, 8cm by 5cm; unbleached with navy flowers, 5cm square. Six-strand embroidery floss No. 25 in cobalt blue. For E: Pink velveteen, 28cm by 16cm. Cotton broadcloth, red with white flowers, 5cm square. Cardboard. For each: Polyester fiberfill.

FINISHED SIZE: See diagrams.

DIRECTIONS:

Cut out pieces adding 0.5cm all around for seam allowance.

A (Actual Size)

Front

Add 0.5cm all around for seam allowance.

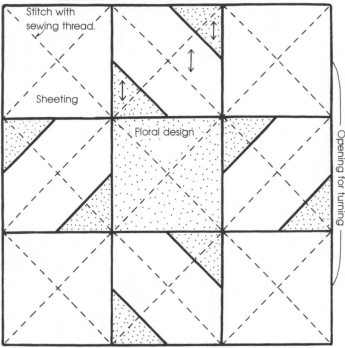

Stitch with sewing thread.

Sheeting

Floral design

Opening for turning

☆ Cut 10cm square from dull mauve for back.

B (Actual Size)

Add 0.5cm all around for seam allowance.

Front

Floral design

Peony rose   Lavender

Stitch with sewing thread.

Back

Floral design

Cut 2.

Opening for turning

For A:

① Sew pieces as shown and stitch along broken lines.

② With right sides facing, sew front and back together leaving one side open for turning. Turn inside out.

③ Stuff with fiberfill and slip-stitch opening closed.

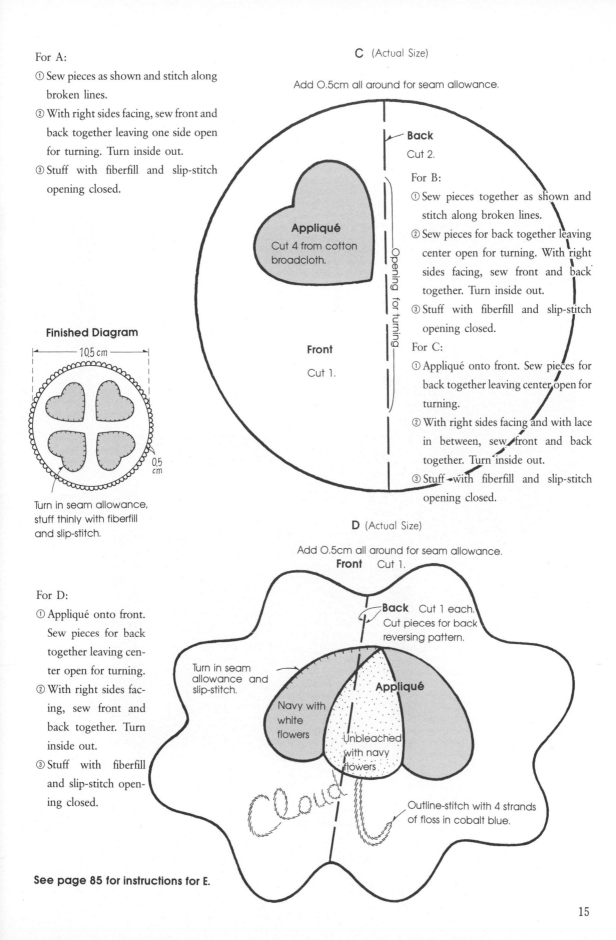

C (Actual Size)

Add 0.5cm all around for seam allowance.

Back
Cut 2.

Opening for turning

For B:

① Sew pieces together as shown and stitch along broken lines.

② Sew pieces for back together leaving center open for turning. With right sides facing, sew front and back together. Turn inside out.

③ Stuff with fiberfill and slip-stitch opening closed.

For C:

① Appliqué onto front. Sew pieces for back together leaving center open for turning.

② With right sides facing and with lace in between, sew front and back together. Turn inside out.

③ Stuff with fiberfill and slip-stitch opening closed.

Front
Cut 1.

Appliqué
Cut 4 from cotton broadcloth.

Finished Diagram

10.5 cm

0.5 cm

Turn in seam allowance, stuff thinly with fiberfill and slip-stitch.

For D:

① Appliqué onto front. Sew pieces for back together leaving center open for turning.

② With right sides facing, sew front and back together. Turn inside out.

③ Stuff with fiberfill and slip-stitch opening closed.

D (Actual Size)

Add 0.5cm all around for seam allowance.

Front   Cut 1.

Back Cut 1 each.
Cut pieces for back reversing pattern.

Turn in seam allowance and slip-stitch.

Appliqué

Navy with white flowers

Unbleached with navy flowers

Cloud

Outline-stitch with 4 strands of floss in cobalt blue.

See page 85 for instructions for E.

Appliquéd Pictures
Instructions on page 18.

Appliquéd Pictures, shown on pages 16 & 17.

MATERIALS:

Cotton broadcloth: For Picture at left: Cream, 28cm by 6cm; light olive green with leaf design, 22cm by 11cm; off-white with blue flowers, 22cm by 8cm; olive green, 22cm by 6cm; coral pink, 16cm by 8cm; green with white dots, 15cm by 13cm; brown, 8cm by 15cm; scraps of rose pink with pink dots, pink with flowers, rose pink and pink checks, gray, and brown. For Picture at center: Light olive green with leaf design, 22cm by 14cm; off-white with blue flowers, 22cm by 9cm; rose pink with pink dots, cream, olive green with flowers, 14cm by 7cm each; green with white dots, 10cm by 9cm; brown, 5cm by 11cm; scraps of coral pink, beige, and white. For Picture at right: Light olive green with

(Actual Size) Add 0.5cm all around for seam allowance unless otherwise indicated.

Left

Green with white dots

Off-white with blue flowers

△

∨

Rose pink with pink dots

Brown

✳

Rose pink and pink checks

Pink with flowers

✳

◎

T

Gray

Dark brown

T

◎

▲

Light olive green with leaf design

∨

Cream

X

X

X

X

X

X

Coral pink

X

X

X

X

X

Olive green

Add 3cm for margin to each piece which is placed at side.

leaf design, 26cm by 8cm; off-white with blue flowers, 22cm by 11cm; pistachio green with flowers, 22cm by 8cm; olive green with flowers, 14cm by 5cm; cream, 18cm by 6cm; scraps of white, green with white dots, olive green, rose pink and pink checks, gray, coral pink, and brown. For each: Six-strand embroidery floss No. 25 in colors matching the appliqués; yellow for picture at center and brown for picture at right. Frame, 15cm square (inside measurement).

FINISHED SIZE: Same size as frame.

DIRECTIONS:

Add 0.5cm all around for seam allowance except pieces which need margin for turning. Sew pieces together along straight lines. Sew curved pieces by hand, using slip stitch and colors matching the appliqués. Outline stitch for girl's hair and for handle.

Center

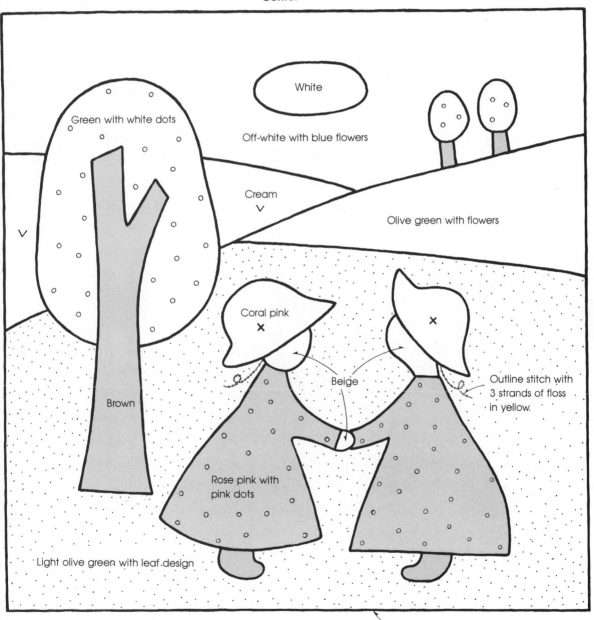

Green with white dots

White

Off-white with blue flowers

Cream
ν

Olive green with flowers

ν

Coral pink
X

Outline stitch with 3 strands of floss in yellow.

Beige

Brown

X

Rose pink with pink dots

Light olive green with leaf design

Add 3cm for margin to each piece which is placed at side.

See page 90 for picture at right.

Brooches
Instructions on page 22.

Pochettes and Shoe Cases
Instructions for Pochettes on page 88 and for Shoe Cases on page 89.

Patchwork Pictures
Instructions on page 106.

MATERIALS:

For Balloon: Scraps of blue cotton broadcloth with dots and red sheeting. Red and yellow rickrack, 0.4cm by 7cm each. Six-strand embroidery floss No. 25 in brown, yellow and blue. Polyester fiberfill. Glue. For Yacht: Scraps of red, yellow and peacock green cotton satin. Six-strand embroidery floss No. 25 in olive green. Polyester fiberfill. Safety pin. For Skillet: Cotton broadcloth: Scraps of navy with white dots, orange print, and white. Scrap of yellow felt. Six-strand embroidery floss No. 25 in cherry pink. White sewing thread, #50. Polyester fiberfill. Glue. For Baby Carriage: Cotton broadcloth: Scraps of blue with white flowers, and pink with white flowers. White cotton lace edging, 1.5cm by 4cm. Six-strand embroidery floss No. 25 in pink. 2 pink buttons, 1.8cm in diameter. Polyester fiberfill. For Ice cream: Scraps of pink cotton fabric and brown gingham checks. Six-strand embroidery floss

Patterns (Actual Size)
Add 0.5cm all around for seam allowance except felt and cut one pair each unless otherwise indicated.

Balloon

6 strands of floss in blue

Opening for turning

Rickrack
Red Yellow

Dots

Glue 6 strands of floss together.

6 strands of floss in yellow

Red

DIRECTIONS: Opening for turning

①Sew rickrack on front of balloon.
②With right sides facing and knotted ends of 6 strands of floss in between, sew front and back together leaving opening for turning. Turn inside out. Stuff thinly with fiberfill. Slip-stitch opening closed.
③With right sides facing and ends of 6 strands of floss in between, sew red pieces together. Turn inside out. Stuff thinly with fiberfill and slip-stitch opening closed.
④Attach bow.

DIRECTIONS:

For Skillet

6 strands of floss
Cherry pink

6 strands of floss
Orange Cut 1.

DIRECTIONS:

①Sew navy and orange pieces together.
②Appliqué white piece onto navy and glue yellow felt onto white.
③With right sides facing, sew front and back together leaving bottom open for turning. Turn inside out. Stuff thinly with fiberfill. Slip-stitch opening closed.
④Quilt along quilting line and attach bow.

Quilt with white sewing thread.

Navy

Felt

White Cut 1.

Opening for turning

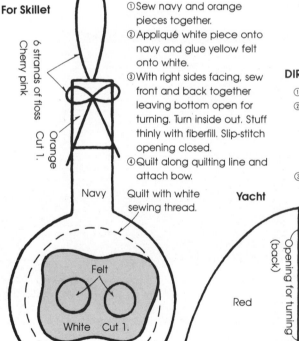

Yacht

Opening for turning (back)

Peacock green

Red

Yellow

Opening for turning

Yellow

Outline-stitch with 3 strands of floss in olive green.

①With right sides facing, sew pieces for sail together leaving opening for turning. Turn inside out. Stuff thinly with fiberfill. Slip-stitch opening closed.
②Outline-stitch on boat. With right sides facing, sew pieces for boat together leaving opening for turning. Turn inside out. Stuff thinly with fiberfill. Slip-stitch opening closed, catching end of pole.
③Attach safety pin onto back.

No. 25 in white and brown. Polyester fiberfill. Safety pin. For Watermelon: Scraps of yellow green gingham checks and red with white dots. Scrap of brown felt. Polyester fiberfill. Safety pin. Glue.

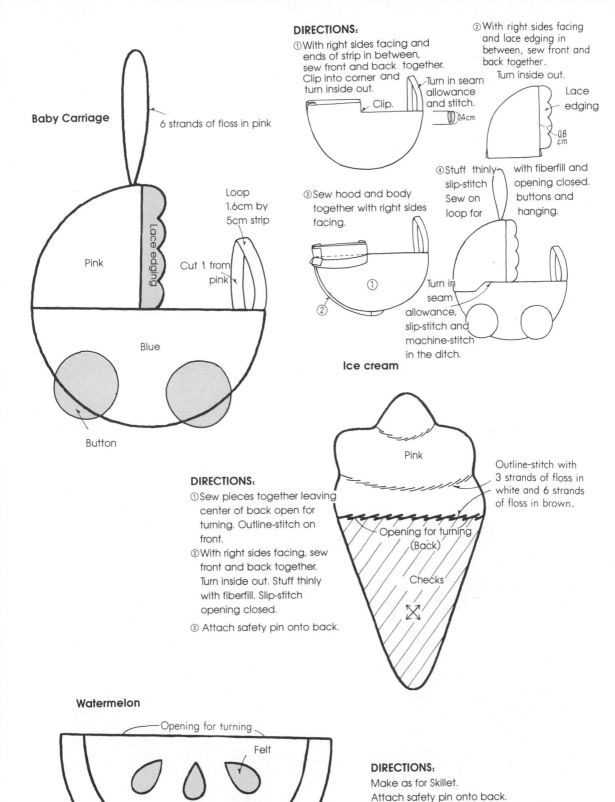

Baby Carriage

6 strands of floss in pink

DIRECTIONS:

①With right sides facing and ends of strip in between, sew front and back together. Clip into corner and turn inside out.

②With right sides facing and lace edging in between, sew front and back together.
Turn inside out.

Clip.

Turn in seam allowance and stitch.
.04cm

Lace edging

0.8 cm

④Stuff thinly slip-stitch Sew on loop for

with fiberfill and opening closed. buttons and hanging.

③Sew hood and body together with right sides facing.

Loop
1.6cm by
5cm strip

Cut 1 from pink

Lace edging

Pink

Blue

Button

①
②

Turn in seam allowance, slip-stitch and machine-stitch in the ditch.

Ice cream

Pink

Outline-stitch with 3 strands of floss in white and 6 strands of floss in brown.

Opening for turning (Back)

Checks

DIRECTIONS:

①Sew pieces together leaving center of back open for turning. Outline-stitch on front.

②With right sides facing, sew front and back together. Turn inside out. Stuff thinly with fiberfill. Slip-stitch opening closed.

③ Attach safety pin onto back.

Watermelon

Opening for turning

Felt

Dots   Cut 1.

Checks

DIRECTIONS:

Make as for Skillet.
Attach safety pin onto back.

Bedspread
Instructions on page 26.

24

Bedspread, *shown on pages 24 & 25.*

MATERIALS:

Cotton broadcloth: Sky blue with flowers, 90cm by 280cm; light blue with flowers, 90cm by 130cm; white with flowers, 75cm by 78cm for (a) and 35cm by 23cm for (b); light blue gray with flowers, 50cm by 40cm; powder green with flowers and lavender with flowers, 40cm by 30cm each; dark blue gray with flowers, 23cm by 17cm; lavender and white stripes, 30cm square; old rose with flowers, 19cm by 16cm. Sheeting: Blue, 90cm by 170cm; gray, 65cm by 18cm; dull mauve, 45cm by 35cm; purple, 44cm square; unbleached, 37cm by 9cm; blue gray, 35cm by 10cm; beige, 31cm by 12cm; rose pink, 30cm square; wine red, 26cm by 20cm; cream, 15cm by 13cm; purple gingham checks, 60cm by 10cm. Quilted fabric, gray with flowers, 90cm by 480cm. Six-strand embroidery floss No. 25 in dark brown, charcoal gray, gray, pink and matching colors for appliqués.

FINISHED SIZE: 177cm by 240cm.

DIRECTIONS:

① Add 1cm all around for seam allowance. Cut pieces as indicated and sew them together. Enlarge appliqué patterns and cut out pieces. Sew appliqué pieces together along straight lines and slip-stitch along curved lines.

② Place pieced top on quilted fabric. Bind edges with strips, each side first and then top and bottom edges.

Strip for Binding

Blue with flowers   Cut 2 each.

Sew strips together to make 231cm for (a) and 177cm for (b).

Diagram

Add 1cm all around for seam allowance.

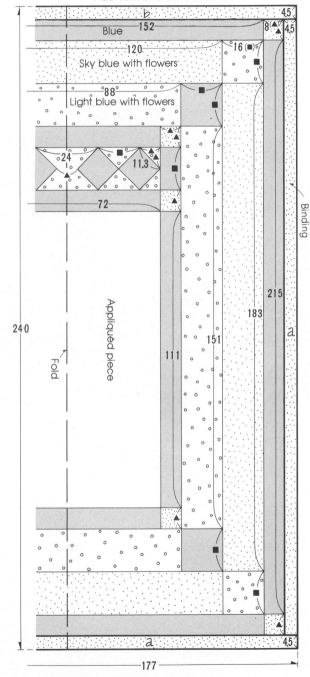

Sew quilted fabric together to make 177cm by 240cm for backing.

Appliqué Patterns

Add 1cm all around for seam allowance.

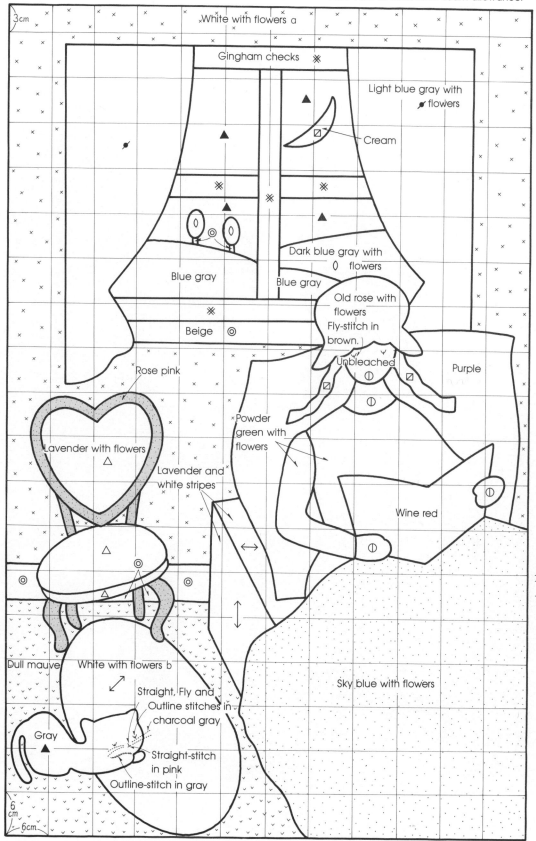

3cm

White with flowers a

Gingham checks ※

Light blue gray with
🌿 flowers

▲

▲

☑ ── Cream

※ ※

▲ ▲

Dark blue gray with
0 flowers

Blue gray   Blue gray

Old rose with
flowers
Fly-stitch in
brown.

※

Beige ◎

Unbleached   Purple

Rose pink

☑   ① ☑

①

Powder
green with
flowers

Lavender with flowers
△

Lavender and
white stripes

Wine red

①

△

↔

◎   ◎
△

①

↕

Dull mauve   White with flowers b
↗

Straight, Fly and
Outline stitches in
charcoal gray

Sky blue with flowers

Gray
▲

Straight-stitch
in pink

Outline-stitch in gray

6
cm
6cm

Use 4 strands of floss for embroidery.
Slip-stitch along curved lines with matching colors
for appliqués.

27

Throw
Instructions on page 31.

Grape Tote Bags, *shown on page 28.*

MATERIALS:

For Bag at left: Quilted fabric in white with pink flowers and sheeting, 74cm by 39cm each. Light wine red cotton broadcloth, 31cm by 16cm. Yellow green felt, 6cm square. Six-strand embroidery floss No. 25 in wine red and sage green. Pink cotton tape, 2.5cm by 130cm. For Bag at right: Pistachio green quilted fabric and cotton broadcloth in same color, 74cm by 39cm each. Yellow green cotton broadcloth, 31cm by 16cm.

Olive green felt, 6cm square. Six-strand embroidery floss No. 25 in sage green and light olive green. Moss green cotton tape, 2.5cm by 130cm. Add 0.5cm to

Appliqué Patterns (Actual Size)

Colors in parentheses are for Bag at left and in brackets for Bag at right.

Quilting line

(Wine red) ⟨Sage green⟩

Use 2 strands of floss.

Outline-stitch

(Sage green)
6 strands of floss ⟨Light olive green⟩
2 strands of floss

Felt

(Yellow green) ⟨Olive green⟩

Slip-stitch.

(Light wine red) ⟨ Yellow green ⟩

Cut 2.

Opening for stuffing
(Make a slit in back piece.)

How to make grapes:

① Cut out 2 pieces for front and back, reversing pattern for back. Make a slit in back piece.

② With right sides facing, sew front and back together. Turn inside out.

③ Stuff thinly with fiberfill and slip-stitch opening closed.

grapes for seam allowance and no seam allowance on leaf.

FINISHED SIZE: See diagram.

DIRECTIONS:

① Place grapes on front of bag and quilt along quilting lines. Appliqué leaf and embroider veins and stems.

② With right sides facing, sew front and back together. Fold each corner as shown matching seams of side and bottom and sew across 6cm to make gusset. Turn to right side.

③ Make inner bag in same manner and insert into outer bag.

④ Turn in seam allowance at top and machine-stitch along edges catching ends of handles.

⑤ Sew on ribbon and tie into bow. ·

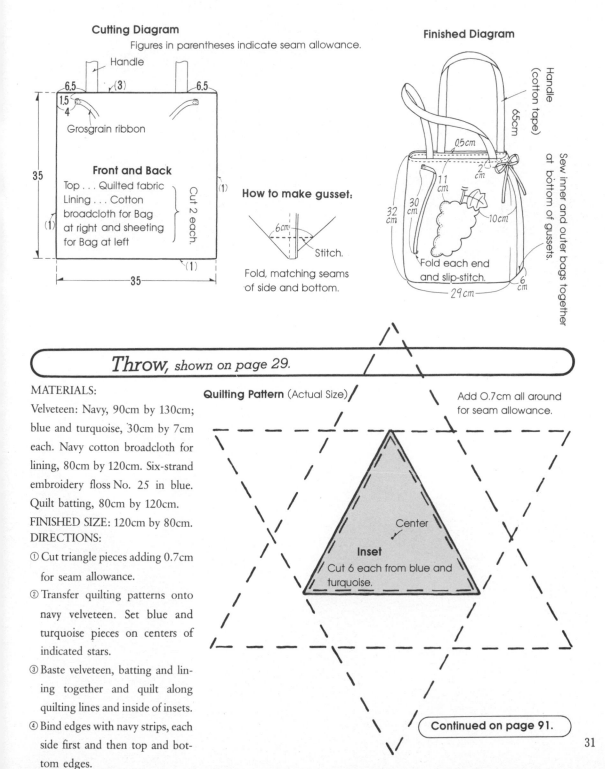

Cutting Diagram

Figures in parentheses indicate seam allowance.

Handle

6.5 (3) 6.5

1.5
4

Grosgrain ribbon

Front and Back

Top . . . Quilted fabric
Lining . . . Cotton broadcloth for Bag at right and sheeting for Bag at left

Cut 2 each.

35

35

(1)

How to make gusset:

6cm

Stitch.

Fold, matching seams of side and bottom.

Finished Diagram

Handle (cotton tape)

65cm

0.5cm

2 cm

11 cm

30 cm

32 cm

10cm

Fold each end and slip-stitch.

6 cm

29cm

Sew inner and outer bags together at bottom of gussets.

Throw, shown on page 29.

MATERIALS:

Velveteen: Navy, 90cm by 130cm; blue and turquoise, 30cm by 7cm each. Navy cotton broadcloth for lining, 80cm by 120cm. Six-strand embroidery floss No. 25 in blue. Quilt batting, 80cm by 120cm.

FINISHED SIZE: 120cm by 80cm.

DIRECTIONS:

① Cut triangle pieces adding 0.7cm for seam allowance.

② Transfer quilting patterns onto navy velveteen. Set blue and turquoise pieces on centers of indicated stars.

③ Baste velveteen, batting and lining together and quilt along quilting lines and inside of insets.

④ Bind edges with navy strips, each side first and then top and bottom edges.

Quilting Pattern (Actual Size)

Add 0.7cm all around for seam allowance.

Center

Inset

Cut 6 each from blue and turquoise.

Continued on page 91.

**Tablecloth
(Left)**
Instructions on
page 34.

**Table Center
(Right)**
Instructions on
page 35.

Tablecloth, *shown on page 32.*

Diagram

Add 1cm all around for seam allowance.

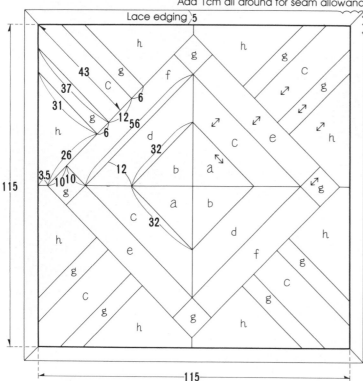

Lace edging 5

115

115

Required amounts of fabric

a	White with light pink dots	34cm square each
b	White with dark pink dots	
c	Rose pink with birds and flowers	58cm by 73cm
d	Pink with white flowers	58cm by 28cm
e	White with flowers	58cm by 24cm each
f	White with bows and flowers	
g	White with pink branches	64cm by 51cm
h	White with pink dots	66cm square

MATERIALS:

Cotton broadcloth: See above list for colors and amounts. White cotton lace edging: 6.5cm by 510cm; 5cm by 350cm; 3.5cm by 150cm with holes to run ribbon through; 2.5cm by 240cm with designs on both edges; 2.5cm by 580cm. Pink satin ribbon, 1cm by 180cm.

FINISHED SIZE: 125cm square.

DIRECTIONS:

① Cut out pieces adding 1cm all around for seam allowance.

② Sew pieces together in numerical order form ① to ④. Place 3.5cm wide lace edging on seam of ① and 2.5cm wide lace edging with designs on both edges on seam of ③. Machine-stitch.

③ Sew corner pieces together placing lace edgings between pieces as shown.

④ Make 3 more corner pieces in same manner. Sew them together to make a big square without center. Sew 6.5cm wide lace edging around outer edges.

⑤ Sew center square and pieced corners together, placing 5cm wide lace edging in between. Tie ribbon into bow and sew in place.

Piecing Diagram

Turn in seam allowance and machine-stitch.

Turn in seam allowance and pieced corners as shown and machine-stitch.

Overlap seam allowances of lace and top-stitch.

Press seam open. Insert ribbon into holes.

Turn seam to one side and top-stitch.

5cm

15cm

3.8cm

Top-stitch.

Turn in ends.

Tie 20cm-long ribbon into bow and sew onto lace at 2 corners.

Table Center, *shown on page 33.*

Diagram Add 1cm all around for seam allowance.

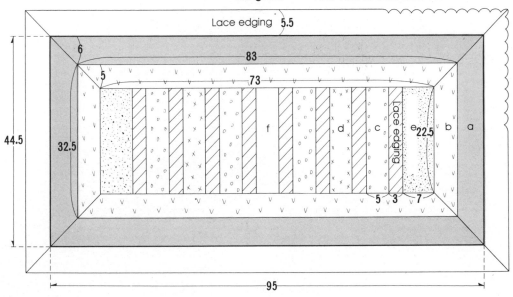

Lace edging 5.5

6

83

5

73

f

d

c

e 22.5

b

a

Lace edging

44.5

32.5

5 3 7

95

MATERIALS:

Cotton broadcloth: (a) White with sky blue dots, 24cm by 97cm; (b) sky blue with cream dots, 85cm by 21cm; (c) sky blue with blue bows and flowers, 28cm by 25cm; (d) white with lavender flowers, 14cm by 25cm; (e) white with sky blue flowers, 18cm by 25cm; (f) white with blue bows and flowers, 7cm by 25cm. White cotton lace edging: 7cm by 335cm; 5cm by 200cm with seam allowance on both sides for insertion; 3.5cm by 210cm with holes for ribbon to run through; 2.5cm by 250cm with designs on both sides. Blue satin ribbon, 1cm by 230cm.

FINISHED SIZE: 106cm by 55.5cm.

DIRECTIONS:

① Cut out pieces adding 1cm all around for seam allowance.

② Sew pieces together in numerical order from ① to ④.

③ Place 2.5cm wide lace edging on seam of ② and 3.5cm wide lace edging on seam of ③. Machine-stitch.

④ Sew on 7cm wide lace edging all around. Tie ribbon into bow and sew in place.

Piecing Diagram

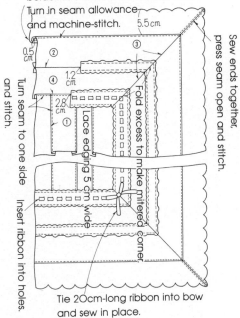

Overlap seam allowances of lace edging and border as shown and machine-stitch.

Turn in seam allowance and machine-stitch. 5.5cm

0.5 cm

②

1.2 cm

④

2.8 cm

①

③

Sew ends together, press seam open and stitch.

Turn seam to one side and stitch.

Fold excess to make mitered corner.

Lace edging 5 cm wide

Insert ribbon into holes.

Tie 20cm-long ribbon into bow and sew in place.

Pillows (Left)
Instructions on page 38.

Telephone Cover and Mat
Instructions on page 38.

Small Mat
Instructions on page 92.

Pillows, shown on page 36.

MATERIALS:

Cotton broadcloth: For Pillow at left: Brown, 46cm by 96cm; for patches (see the list below for colors and designs), (a) 43cm by 9cm, (b) 34cm by 9cm, (c) 26cm by 9cm (d) 17cm by 9cm, (e) 9cm square. For Pillow at right: Light brown, 46cm by 96cm. For patches, the required amounts are the same but use different colors and designs as shown in the list below. Six-strand embroidery floss No. 25 in mustard for pillow at left and brown for pillow at right. 40cm long zipper. Inner pillow stuffed with kapok, 45cm square.

FINISHED SIZE: 44cm square.

DIRECTIONS:

① Outline-stitch horizontally and vertically on front with 4 strands of floss as shown in the diagram. Slip-stitch patch pieces onto indicated places.

② Sew zipper onto back pieces. With right sides facing, sew front and back together. Turn inside out. Insert inner pillow into outer pillow.

Add 1cm all around for seam allowance unless otherwise indicated.

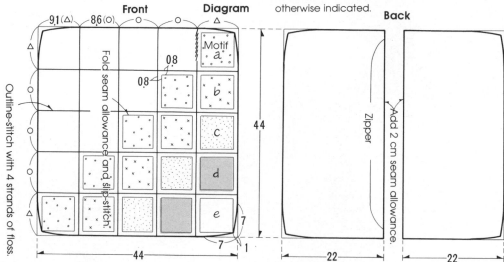

Patch

Add 0.7cm all around for seam allowance.

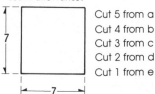

Cut 5 from a
Cut 4 from b
Cut 3 from c
Cut 2 from d
Cut 1 from e

Color Key for Patches

	Pillow at left	Pillow at right
a	Beige	Brown with buds
b	Unbleached with flowers	Dark brown with flowers
c	Beige with flowers	Beige with blue flowers
d	Brown with flowers	Light brown with flowers
e	Brown with buds	Beige

Telephone Cover and Mat, shown on page 37.

MATERIALS:

For Mat: Unbleached soft denim, 27cm in diameter. White felt for lining, 25.5cm in diameter. 8 kinds of prints of cotton broadcloth for patches (see photo), 12cm by 5cm each. For cover: Unbleached soft denim, 46cm by 39cm. Cotton broadcloth for lining, 39cm in diameter. 8 kinds of prints of cotton broadcloth for patches (same as Mat), 15cm by 17cm each. Six-strand

embroidery floss No. 25 in ivory for Mat, and ivory, yellow green and lavender for Cover. Yellow green cotton tape, 1.5cm by 45cm.

FINISHED SIZE: Mat, 25.5cm in diameter. Cover, 37cm in diameter.

DIRECTIONS:

Follow individual instructions shown on next page.

Cutting Diagram

Add 0.7cm all around for seam allowance.

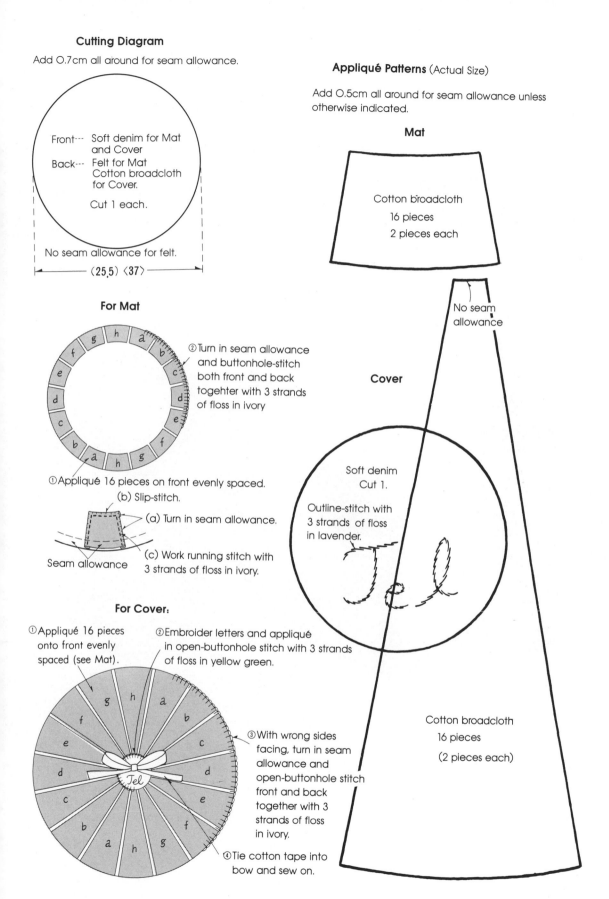

Front--- Soft denim for Mat and Cover

Back--- Felt for Mat
Cotton broadcloth for Cover.

Cut 1 each.

No seam allowance for felt.

|— (25.5) ⟨37⟩ —|

Appliqué Patterns (Actual Size)

Add 0.5cm all around for seam allowance unless otherwise indicated.

Mat

Cotton broadcloth
16 pieces
2 pieces each

No seam allowance

Cover

Soft denim
Cut 1.

Outline-stitch with 3 strands of floss in lavender.

Cotton broadcloth
16 pieces
(2 pieces each)

For Mat

② Turn in seam allowance and buttonhole-stitch both front and back togehter with 3 strands of floss in ivory

① Appliqué 16 pieces on front evenly spaced.

(b) Slip-stitch.

(a) Turn in seam allowance.

Seam allowance

(c) Work running stitch with 3 strands of floss in ivory.

For Cover:

① Appliqué 16 pieces onto front evenly spaced (see Mat).

② Embroider letters and appliqué in open-buttonhole stitch with 3 strands of floss in yellow green.

③ With wrong sides facing, turn in seam allowance and open-buttonhole stitch front and back together with 3 strands of floss in ivory.

④ Tie cotton tape into bow and sew on.

Ⓐ

Ⓓ

3: Kitche

Tray Mats and Coasters
Instructions on page 42.

Dishcloths
Instructions on page 94.

Tray Mats, *shown on pages 40 & 41.*

For Round Mat:

MATERIALS:

Unbleached quilted fabric and cotton print in blue with white flowers, 35cm square each. Blue bias tape, 1.8cm by 112cm.

FINISHED SIZE: 35cm in diameter.

Cutting Diagram

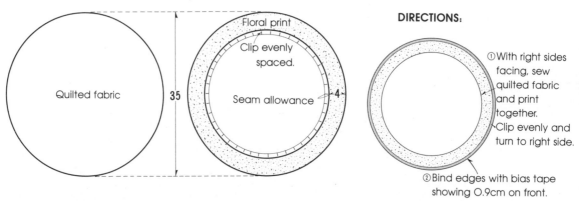

DIRECTIONS:

①With right sides facing, sew quilted fabric and print together. Clip evenly and turn to right side.

②Bind edges with bias tape showing 0.9cm on front.

For Square Mat:

MATERIALS:

Heavyweight white cotton fabric, 34cm by 19cm. Cotton broadcloth: Blue with white flowers, 81cm by 12cm; white with blue flowers, 65cm by 10cm; white for lining, 46cm by 31cm. Blue bias tape, 1.8cm by 158cm.

FINISHED SIZE: 46cm by 31cm.

Cutting Diagram   Add 1cm all around for seam allowance
Front   unless otherwise indicated.

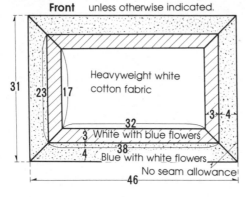

DIRECTIONS:

①Sew pieces together for front.

②With right sides facing, bind edges with bias tape showing 0.9cm on front.

Turn in end.

Coasters, *shown on pages 40 & 41.*

MATERIALS:

For A: Cotton broadcloth: Navy, 24cm by 12cm; Blue with flowers, 10cm by 9cm; peacock green, 30cm square. For B: Lavender gingham checks, 24cm by 12cm. Cotton broadcloth: Purple with white flowers, 30cm square; wine red, 9cm by 5cm; rose, 5cm square. For C: Cotton broadcloth: blue with white flowers, 19cm by 12cm; white with doll design, 7cm square. Blue cotton fabric, 17cm by 7cm. Navy and white checks, 30cm square. For D: Cotton broadcloth: Blue gray, 24cm by 12cm; lavender with light purple flowers, 10cm square; peacock green, 30cm square. For E: Gotton broadcloth: Green, 24cm by 12cm; white with black dots, 8cm square; navy with white flowers, 4cm square; navy, 30cm square. White sewing thread, #50. Six-strand embroidery floss No. 25 in navy for D. Quilt batting, 12cm square for each.

FINISHED SIZE: 12cm in diameter.

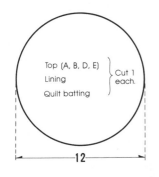

Top (A, B, D, E)
Lining
Quilt batting } Cut 1 each.

— 12 —

	A	B	C	D	E
Top	Navy	Gingham checks		Blue gray	Green
Lining	Same	Same	Floral design	Same	Same
Strip for binding	Peacock green	Floral design	Checks	Peacock green	Navy

Strip for Binding

2.5

— 39 —

Appliqué Patterns (Actual Size)

Add 0.5cm all around for seam allowance unless otherwise indicated.

DIRECTIONS FOR TOP:

For A:

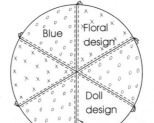

Slip-stitch.
Quilt with sewing thread.
Straight st. with sewing thread.
2cm

Turn in seam allowance of appliqué piece and slip-stitch onto top. Place top on batting and quilt.

For B:

| Wine red | Rose |
| Floral design | Wine red |

Slip-stitch on.
Quilt with sewing thread.

Sew pieces together and turn seams to one side. Turn in seam allowance and appliqué onto top. Place top on batting and quilt.

For C:

Blue Floral design Doll design
Quilt with sewing thread.

Sew 6 pieces together and turn seams to one side. Place top on batting and quilt.

For D:

1.5cm
Slip-stitch
Star
Quilt with sewing thread.

Embroider letters on appliqué piece. Turn in seam allowance and appliqué onto top. Place top on batting and quilt.

For E:

Make as for B.

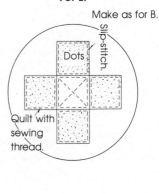

Dots
Slip-stitch.
Quilt with sewing thread.

A

Floral design

No seam allowance

B

Wine red   Cut 2.
Rose
Floral design   Cut 1 each.

C

Blue --------- Cut 3.
Floral design --- Cut 2.
Doll design --- Cut 1.

D

Floral design

Star

Outline-stitch with 2 strands of floss in navy.

E

White dots
------ Cut 4.
Floral design
------ Cut 1.

DIRECTIONS:

Cut out pieces as indicated and appliqué on top. With wrong sides facing, bind edges of top and lining together with bias-cut strip showing 0.6cm on front.

Curtain and Potholders

Instructions for Curtain on page 96
and for Potholders on page 46.

Lunch Bags, Cooker Cover and Napkins
Instructions for Lunch Bags on page 97,
for Cooker Cover on page 98
and for Napkins on page 99.

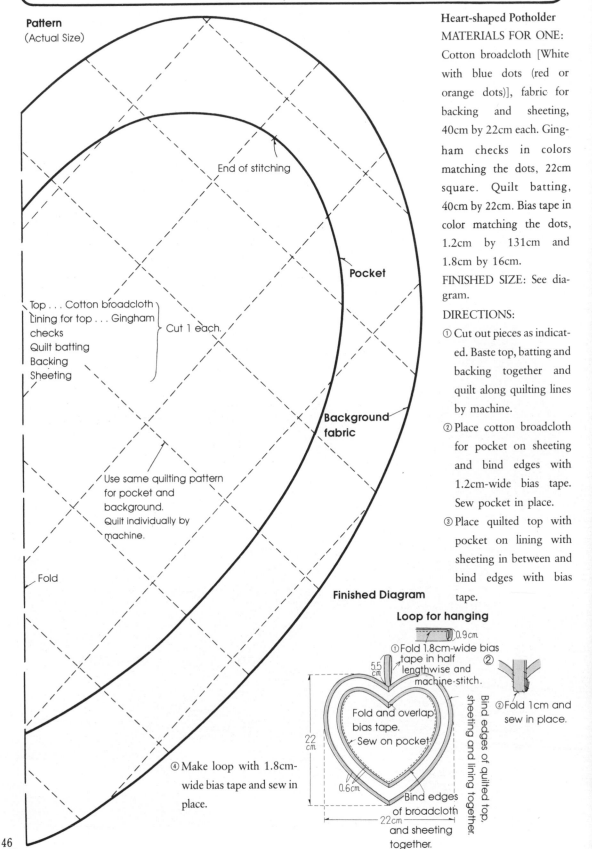

Potholders, *shown on page 44.*

Pattern
(Actual Size)

End of stitching

Pocket

Top . . . Cotton broadcloth
Lining for top . . . Gingham
checks
Quilt batting
Backing
Sheeting

Cut 1 each.

Use same quilting pattern
for pocket and
background.
Quilt individually by
machine.

Background
fabric

Fold

Finished Diagram

④ Make loop with 1.8cm-
wide bias tape and sew in
place.

Heart-shaped Potholder
MATERIALS FOR ONE:
Cotton broadcloth [White with blue dots (red or orange dots)], fabric for backing and sheeting, 40cm by 22cm each. Gingham checks in colors matching the dots, 22cm square. Quilt batting, 40cm by 22cm. Bias tape in color matching the dots, 1.2cm by 131cm and 1.8cm by 16cm.

FINISHED SIZE: See diagram.

DIRECTIONS:
① Cut out pieces as indicated. Baste top, batting and backing together and quilt along quilting lines by machine.
② Place cotton broadcloth for pocket on sheeting and bind edges with 1.2cm-wide bias tape. Sew pocket in place.
③ Place quilted top with pocket on lining with sheeting in between and bind edges with bias tape.

Loop for hanging

0.9cm
① Fold 1.8cm-wide bias tape in half lengthwise and machine-stitch.

②
② Fold 1cm and sew in place.

5.5 cm

Fold and overlap
bias tape.
Sew on pocket.

22 cm

0.6cm

Bind edges of quilted top, sheeting and lining together.

Bind edges
of broadcloth
and sheeting
together.

22cm

46

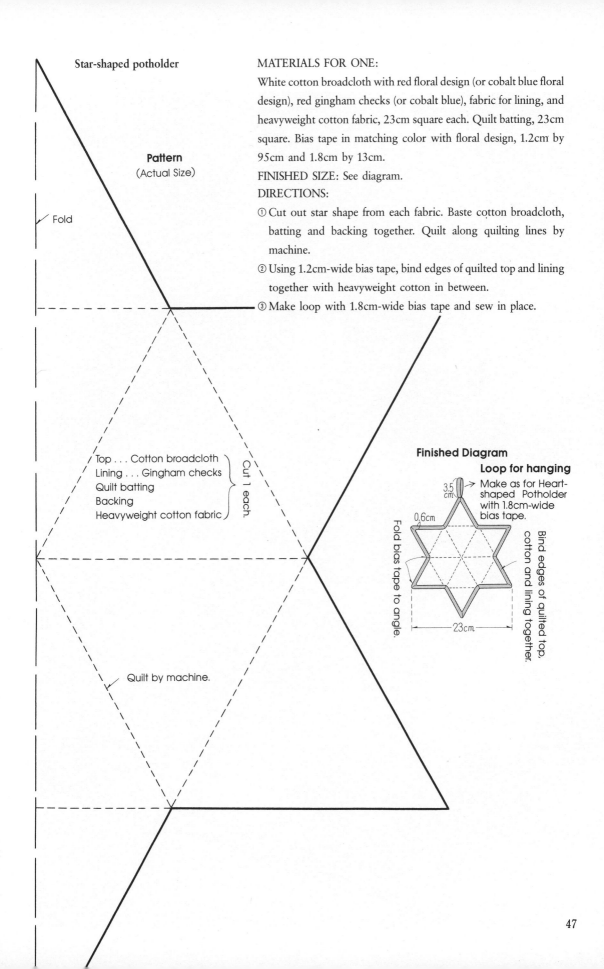

Star-shaped potholder

Pattern
(Actual Size)

Fold

Top . . . Cotton broadcloth
Lining . . . Gingham checks
Quilt batting
Backing
Heavyweight cotton fabric

Cut 1 each.

Quilt by machine.

MATERIALS FOR ONE:
White cotton broadcloth with red floral design (or cobalt blue floral design), red gingham checks (or cobalt blue), fabric for lining, and heavyweight cotton fabric, 23cm square each. Quilt batting, 23cm square. Bias tape in matching color with floral design, 1.2cm by 95cm and 1.8cm by 13cm.

FINISHED SIZE: See diagram.

DIRECTIONS:

① Cut out star shape from each fabric. Baste cotton broadcloth, batting and backing together. Quilt along quilting lines by machine.

② Using 1.2cm-wide bias tape, bind edges of quilted top and lining together with heavyweight cotton in between.

③ Make loop with 1.8cm-wide bias tape and sew in place.

Finished Diagram

Loop for hanging

Make as for Heart-shaped Potholder with 1.8cm-wide bias tape.

3.5 cm

0.6cm

Fold bias tape to angle.

Bind edges of quilted top, cotton and lining together.

23cm

Shelf Mats
Instructions on page 50.

Table Center, *shown on page 48.*

MATERIALS:

Cotton broadcloth: Light pink, 77cm by 43cm; dark pink, 76cm by 12cm. Cotton prints (see photo for colors and designs), 48 pieces of 14cm by 6cm each. Lavender sheeting for lining, 75cm by 49cm. White sewing thread, #30. Quilt batting, 73cm by 47cm.

FINISHED SIZE: 73cm by 47cm.

DIRECTIONS:

① Cut out patch pieces adding 0.7cm all around for seam allowance. Sew pieces together and appliqué onto ground in slip stitch. Appliqué light pink pieces in place.

② Sew purple and dark pink strips all around. With right sides facing, sew top and lining together leaving opening for turning. Place quilt batting on wrong side and turn to right side. Slip-stitch opening closed.

③ Quilt along quilting lines.

Appliqué Patterns

Add 0.7cm all around for seam allowance.

Cut 4 from light pink.

Cut one from light pink.

Cut 48 from prints!

Quilt with sewing thread.

Diagram

Add 0.7 cm seam allowance.

73

1.5

1.8

2

2

47

4

Cotton print Center

Background fabric
Light pink

Dark pink

Purple

41

Slip-stitch

Quilt with sewing thread.

67

Shelf Mats, *shown on page 49.*

MATERIALS:

Cotton broadcloth: For Mat at top: Lavender with cream dots, 88cm by 48cm; purple, 70cm by 22cm; white, 35cm by 5cm. For Mat at center: Rose pink, 88cm by 48cm; lavender with cream dots, 70cm by 22cm; purple, 30cm by 5cm. For Mat at bottom: Lavender with cream dots, 88cm by 48cm; purple,

70cm by 22cm; powder green, 35cm by 5cm. Quilt batting, 66cm by 23cm for each.

FINISHED SIZE: See diagram.

DIRECTIONS:

Cut out pieces as indicated. Make up for Mat following instructions shown on next page.

Cutting Diagram

Figures in parentheses indicate seam allowance.
Add no seam allowance unless otherwise indicated.

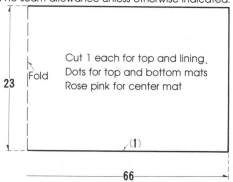

23

Fold

Cut 1 each for top and lining.
Dots for top and bottom mats
Rose pink for center mat

(1)

66

Strip for binding

Purple for top and bottom mats
Dots for center mat

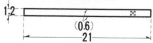

1.6

(0.8)

a = **66** (Cut 1.)
b = **25** (Cut 2.)

Strip for binding (for scalloped edges)

Purple for top and bottom mats
Dots for center mat

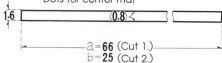

1.2

(0.6)
21

For scalloped border

Cut 6.

Use same fabric as top.

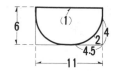

6

(1)

2 4
4.5
11

Appliqué Patterns (Actual Size)

Add 0.5cm all around for seam allowance.

Cut 12 pieces each from white for top mat and
from powder green for bottom mat.

Cut 6 pieces from purple
for center mat.

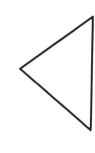

Finished Diagram

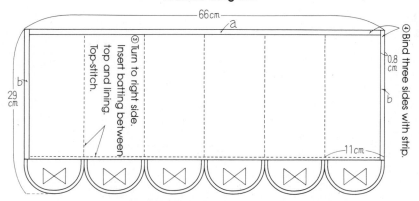

66cm

a

③ Turn to right side.
Insert batting between
top and lining.
Top-stitch.

④ Bind three sides with strip.

0.8 cm

b

29 cm

b

11cm

② With right sides facing and 6 scallops in between,
sew top and lining together.

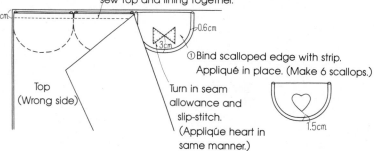

1cm

Top
(Wrong side)

0.6cm

3cm

① Bind scalloped edge with strip.
Appliqué in place. (Make 6 scallops.)

Turn in seam
allowance and
slip-stitch.
(Appliqué heart in
same manner.)

1.5cm

Tea Cozy
Instructions on page 54.

Bottle Covers
Instructions on page 55.

Wall Hanging with Big Pocket
Instructions on page 100.

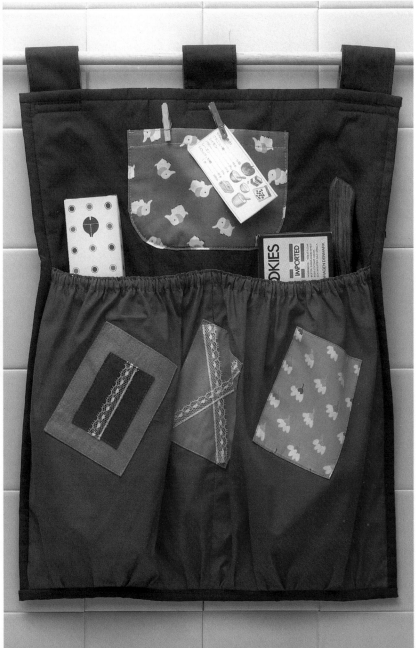

Tea Cozy, *shown on page 52.*

MATERIALS:

Cream quilted fabric, 72cm by 29cm. Cotton broadcloth: Sky blue, 70cm by 5cm; old rose, 15cm square; lavender, 15cm by 5cm; navy with white dots, 10cm by 6cm. Six-strand embroidery floss No. 25 in navy, olive green, rose pink and wine red. Quilt batting, 10cm by 2cm. White cotton lace edging, 1.5cm by 28cm. Lavender rickrack, 0.4cm by 87cm. Bias tape, 1.2cm by 85cm.

FINISHED SIZE: See diagram.

DIRECTIONS:

① Cut out pieces adding 1cm all around for seam allowance except bottom edge. Sew rickrack onto front.

② Sew lace edging and lavender strip onto heart. Embroider letters and slip-stitch heart onto front. Embroider flowers.

③ Embroider flowers on back.

④ With right sides facing and ends of loop in between, sew front and back together. Bind raw edges with bias tape. Turn to right side.

⑤ Bind bottom edge with blue strip.

Appliqué Pattern (Actual Size)

Add 0.7cm all around for seam allowance.

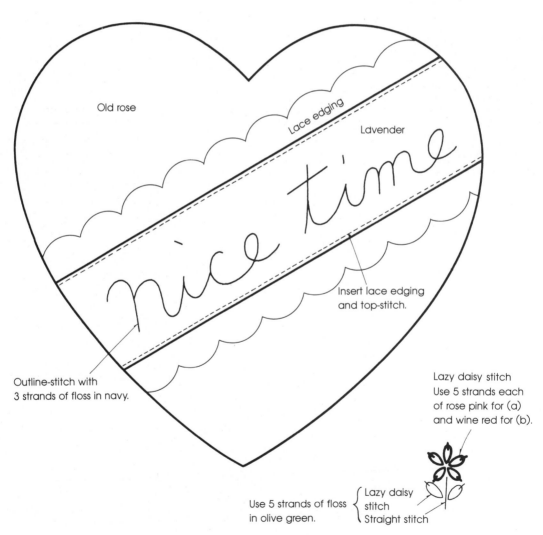

Old rose

Lace edging

Lavender

Insert lace edging and top-stitch.

Outline-stitch with 3 strands of floss in navy.

Lazy daisy stitch
Use 5 strands each of rose pink for (a) and wine red for (b).

Use 5 strands of floss in olive green.

Lazy daisy stitch
Straight stitch

54

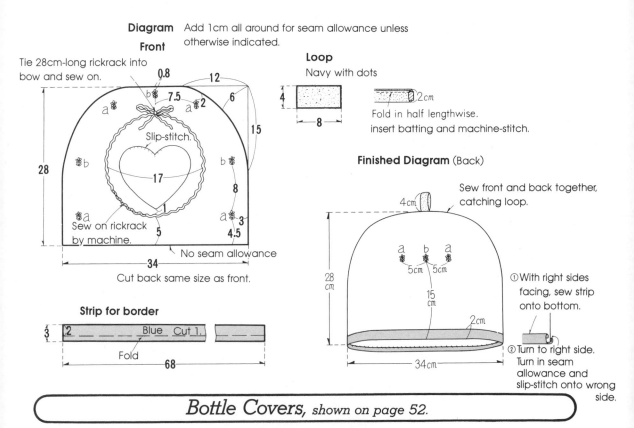

Diagram Add 1cm all around for seam allowance unless otherwise indicated.

Front

Tie 28cm-long rickrack into bow and sew on.

0.8
12
b
7.5
a 2
6
a
15
28
b
17
8
b
Slip-stitch.
a
1
a 3
Sew on rickrack by machine.
5
4.5
No seam allowance
34
Cut back same size as front.

Loop
Navy with dots

4
8
2cm
Fold in half lengthwise.
insert batting and machine-stitch.

Finished Diagram (Back)

Sew front and back together, catching loop.

4cm
a b a
5cm 5cm
28 cm
15 cm
2cm
34cm

① With right sides facing, sew strip onto bottom.

② Turn to right side. Turn in seam allowance and slip-stitch onto wrong side.

Strip for border

3
2
Blue   Cut 1.
Fold
68

Bottle Covers, shown on page 52.

MATERIALS:

For Strawberry Cover: Heavyweight white cotton fabric and light brown gingham checks, 15cm square each. Scrap of red cotton broadcloth. Six-strand embroidery floss, No. 25 in navy, olive green, mustard, yellow green and red. Yellow green satin ribbon, 0.6cm by 42cm. White lace edging, 2cm by 60cm. Elastic tape, 18cm. For Cherry Cover: Heavyweight white cotton fabric and light brown gingham checks, 15cm square each. Scrap of wine red cotton broadcloth. Six-strand embroidery floss No. 25 in purple, navy, rose, dark brown, olive green, moss green and wine red. Sky blue satin ribbon, 0.6cm by 42cm. White cotton lace edging, 2cm by 60cm. Round elastic tape, 18cm. For Blackberry Cover: Cotton broadcloth: White with purple flowers and lavender, 19cm square each; white and lavender stripes, 8cm by 9cm; scraps of purple and green. Six-strand embroidery floss No. 25 in dark brown, moss green, olive green, green, purple and navy. Sky blue satin ribbon, 0.6cm by 50cm. Purple bias tape, 1.2cm by 60cm. Round elastic tape, 20cm.

FINISHED SIZE: See diagrams.

DIRECTIONS:

Cut out pieces adding 0.8cm for seam allowance. Make up for Cover following individual instructions.

Diagram

For Covers with Strawberry and Cherry

Top . . . Heavyweight white cotton fabric ⎱ Cut 1 each adding 0.8cm
Lining . . . Gingham checks ⎰ all around for seam allowance.

For Cover with Blackberry

Top . . . White with purple flowers ⎱ Cut 1 each.
Lining . . . Lavender ⎰

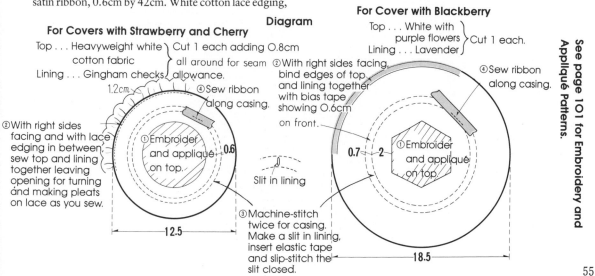

1.2cm
④ Sew ribbon along casing.

② With right sides facing and with lace edging in between, sew top and lining together leaving opening for turning and making pleats on lace as you sew.

① Embroider and appliqué on top.
0.6

12.5

② With right sides facing, bind edges of top and lining together with bias tape showing 0.6cm on front.

Slit in lining

0.7   2

① Embroider and appliqué on top.

④ Sew ribbon along casing.

③ Machine-stitch twice for casing. Make a slit in lining, insert elastic tape and slip-stitch the slit closed.

18.5

See page 101 for Embroidery and Appliqué Patterns.

55

4:CHILDREN'S ROOM

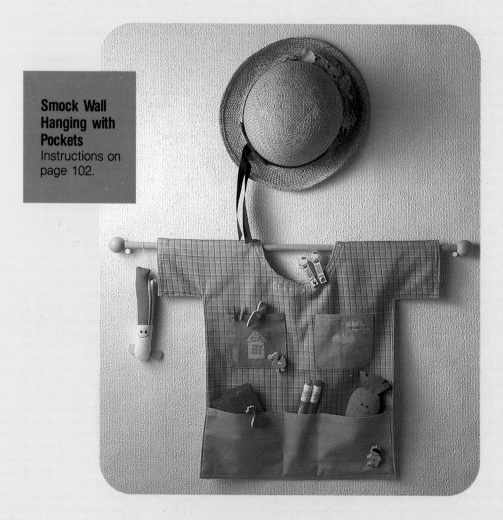

Smock Wall Hanging with Pockets
Instructions on page 102.

Bedspread with Clowns
Instructions on page 58.

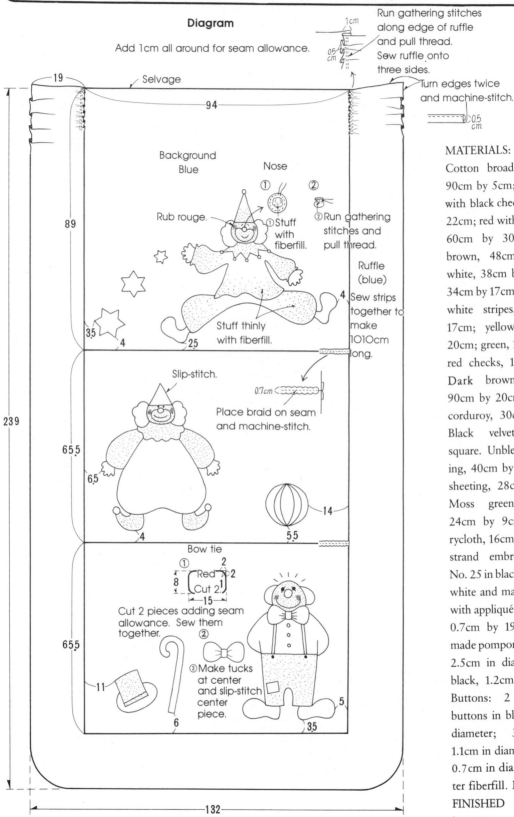

Diagram

Add 1cm all around for seam allowance.

1cm

0.5 cm

Run gathering stitches along edge of ruffle and pull thread.
Sew ruffle onto three sides.

Turn edges twice and machine-stitch.

0.5 cm

19

Selvage

94

89

Background Blue

Nose

① ②

Rub rouge.

①Stuff with fiberfill.

②Run gathering stitches and pull thread.

Ruffle (blue)

4 Sew strips together to make 1010cm long.

239

35 4

25

Stuff thinly with fiberfill.

Slip-stitch.

65.5

6.5

0.7cm

Place braid on seam and machine-stitch.

14

4

5.5

65.5

Bow tie

① 2

8 Red 2

Cut 2.

15

Cut 2 pieces adding seam allowance. Sew them together.

②

③Make tucks at center and slip-stitch center piece.

11

6

5

3.5

132

MATERIALS:
Cotton broadcloth: Blue, 90cm by 5cm; unbleached with black checks, 90cm by 22cm; red with white dots, 60cm by 30cm; golden brown, 48cm by 11cm; white, 38cm by 9cm; red, 34cm by 17cm; red and off-white stripes, 32cm by 17cm; yellow, 30cm by 20cm; green, 16cm square; red checks, 10cm square. Dark brown corduroy, 90cm by 20cm. Vermilion corduroy, 30cm by 9cm. Black velveteen, 30cm square. Unbleached sheeting, 40cm by 13cm. Beige sheeting, 28cm by 10cm. Moss green terrycloth, 24cm by 9cm. Pink terrycloth, 16cm by 6cm. Six-strand embroidery floss No. 25 in black, red, yellow, white and matching color with appliqué pieces. Braid 0.7cm by 192cm. Ready-made pompon: 2 vermilion, 2.5cm in diameter and black, 1.2cm in diameter. Buttons: 2 semicircular buttons in black, 1.2cm in diameter; 3 off-white 1.1cm in diameter; 4 black 0.7cm in diameter. Polyester fiberfill. Rouge.
FINISHED SIZE: 132cm by 239cm.

DIRECTIONS:

① Cut out pieces for background and ruffle adding 1cm all around for seam allowance. Sew pieces of ruffle together to make 1010cm long. Sew pieces for background together to make 220cm long. Make hem for ruffle.

② Enlarge appliqué patterns. Cut out appliqué pieces adding 0.7cm for seam allowance. Appliqué onto background fabric in slip stitch. Pad thinly with fiber-fill as indicated.

③ Place braid on seams of background fabric and stitch. Gather ruffle and baste onto background fabric. Machine-stitch. Remove basting stitches.

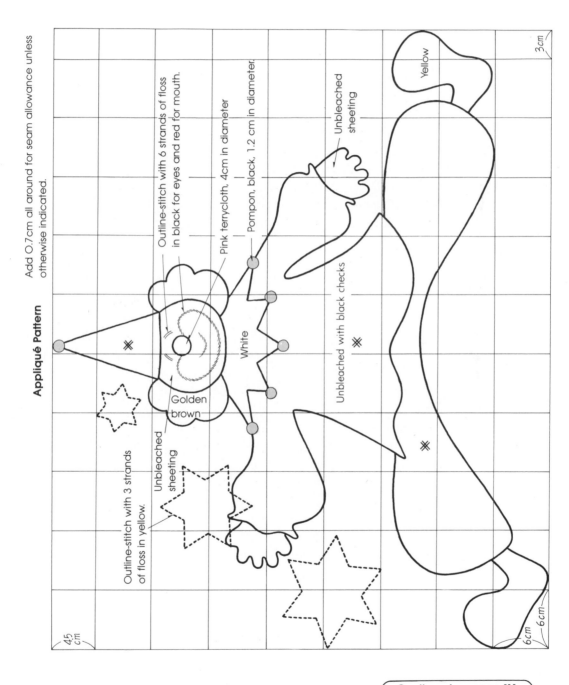

Appliqué Pattern

Add 0.7cm all around for seam allowance unless otherwise indicated.

Outline-stitch with 6 strands of floss in black for eyes and red for mouth.

Pink terrycloth, 4cm in diameter

Pompon, black, 1.2 cm in diameter.

Unbleached sheeting

Yellow

Unbleached with black checks

White

Golden brown

Outline-stitch with 3 strands of floss in yellow.

Unbleached sheeting

3cm

4.5 cm

6cm 6cm

Continued on page 111.

59

4:CHILDREN'S ROOM

**Stuffed Animals
(Rabbit and Cat)**
Instructions on
page 62.

**Dolls
(Boy and Girl)**
Instructions on
page 108.

Stuffed Animals, *shown on page 60.*

MATERIALS:

For Rabbit: Cotton jersey: Ivory, 45cm by 15cm; pink, 12cm by 7cm. Pink cotton broadcloth. Scraps of felt in orange, cream and powder green. White cotton lace edging, 1.5cm by 18cm. Glue. For Cat: Cotton jersey: Beige, 45cm by 15cm; pink, 10cm by 7cm; ivory, 5cm square. Scrap of blue cotton broadcloth. Pearl cotton, #5 in brown. Six-strand embroidery floss No. 25 in white and beige. For each: White sewing thread. Two black beads, 0.5cm in diameter. One brown bead, 0.4cm in diameter. Polyester fiberfill. Rouge. Black felt-tipped pen.

FINISHED SIZE: See diagrams.

DIRECTIONS:

① Cut out pieces adding 0.5cm all around for seam allowance unless otherwise indicated. Note that the grain of head differs from that of body.

② With right sides facing, sew front and back of head together. Make a slit and turn to right side. Stuff with fiberfill.

For Rabbit

Opening for stuffing

Back

Pull thread.

Polyester fiberfill

Pull thread.

Polyester fiberfill

Stuff fiberfill into legs and machine-stitch across body.

④ Nose

0.5cm

Run gathering stitches.

Stuff with fiberfill and pull thread.

1.5cm / 1.3cm / 2.3cm / 23cm / 1.5cm

Tie center of nose with sewing thread and attach brown bead.

⑤ Tail

For Rabbit

For Cat

1.8cm

Stuff with fiberfill and pull thread.

Run gathering stitches.

Sew pieces together with right sides facing. Turn inside out.

⑥ Sew head onto body.

Fold legs from seam and sew onto body.

Match openings of head and body, and overcast.

③ With right sides facing, sew ear pieces together. Turn inside out. Stretch a little as you sew.

Pink (Right side)

For Cat

1 cm

Take stitch to shape sides.

Cut off 0.5cm from raw edge.

0.5cm

How to sew ears

Ear Ivory

Head Front

2cm / 1.5cm

Back

4cm

Turn in seam allowance and slip-stitch onto head.

Seam

Run gathering stitches around opening and pull thread to close.

For Rabbit

Sew on beads for eyes and then draw eyelashes with felt-tipped pen.

Sew center of flower onto head.

Rub rouge. Sew nose and hand onto face individually.

12 cm

4cm

Sew nose and hand onto face individually.

Sew ends of bib onto shoulders.

Glue carrot onto bib.

How to make bib

(Right side)

Lace edging (Wrong side)

0.8cm / 0.5cm

Sew gathered lace edging around edge. Turn seam toward center.

For Cat

Attach eyes and nose as for Cat.

4cm

12 cm

Rub rouge

Straight-stitch with 2 strands of floss in dark brown.

Sew fish onto right hand. Sew fish and left hand onto face.

How to make fish

Turn in seam allowance and work open-buttonhole stitch with 2 strands of floss in white. Stuff with fiberfill.

How to attach eyes

Insert needle at seam of back neck and bring it out at the place for eye. Thread bead onto needle and bring needle out from seam pulling thread tightly to form hollow around eyes.

Sew tail onto back

How to sew ears

Head Front Seam

Ear Beige

Back

0.2cm

Sew ears along seam of head in open-buttonhole stitch with 2 strands of floss in beige.

Take a stitch on back side.

Sew tail onto back.

Patterns (Actual Size)

Add 0.5cm all around for seam allowance
unless otherwise indicated.
After sewing pieces together, trim edges
0.3cm from seam.

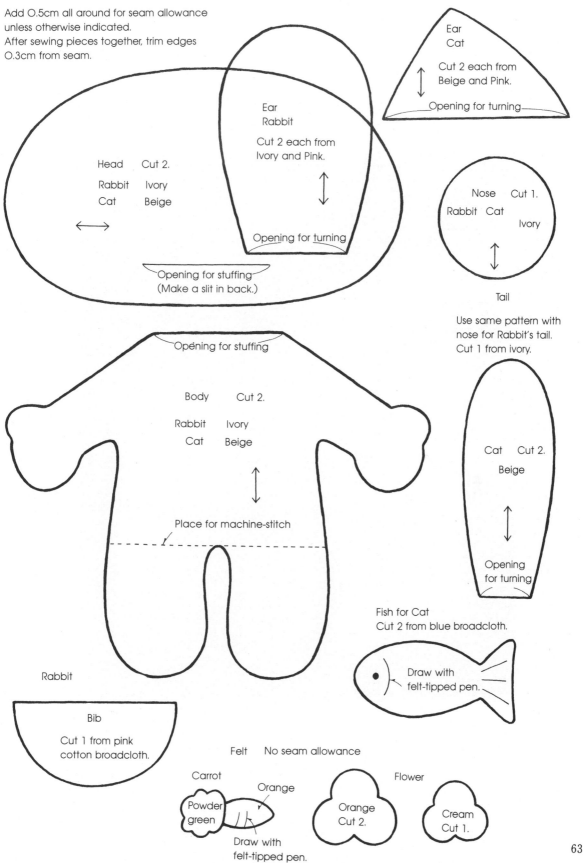

Ear
Cat

Cut 2 each from
Beige and Pink.

Opening for turning

Ear
Rabbit

Cut 2 each from
Ivory and Pink.

Opening for turning

Head   Cut 2.

Rabbit   Ivory
Cat   Beige

Opening for stuffing
(Make a slit in back.)

Nose   Cut 1.

Rabbit   Cat
         Ivory

Tail

Use same pattern with
nose for Rabbit's tail.
Cut 1 from ivory.

Opening for stuffing

Body   Cut 2.

Rabbit   Ivory
Cat   Beige

Place for machine-stitch

Cat   Cut 2.
        Beige

Opening
for turning

Rabbit

Fish for Cat
Cut 2 from blue broadcloth.

Draw with
felt-tipped pen.

Bib

Cut 1 from pink
cotton broadcloth.

Felt   No seam allowance

Carrot

Powder
green

Orange

Draw with
felt-tipped pen.

Flower

Orange
Cut 2.

Cream
Cut 1.

63

4:CHILDREN'S ROOM

Terrycloth Toys (Rabbit, Cat and Bear)
Instructions on page 66.

Tote Bags and Pochettes
Instructions for Pochettes on page 113 and for Tote Bags on page 114.

Terrycloth Toys, *shown on page 64.*

MATERIALS:

Terrycloth: Pink for Rabbit, salmon pink for Cat, and light orange for Bear, 90cm by 15cm each. Cotton broadcloth: Rose pink for Rabbit, red brown for Cat and orange for Bear, 5.5cm in diameter each. Crinkled fabric: Off-white for Rabbit, light brown for Cat and moss green for Bear, 37cm by 9cm each. For each: Two black beads. Polyester fiberfill. Pink felt for Rabbit, 14cm by 9cm.

FINISHED SIZE: See diagrams.

DIRECTIONS:

① Cut out pieces adding 0.5cm all around for seam allowance.

② With right sides facing and felt padding on top, sew ear pieces together leaving bottom open. Turn to right side.

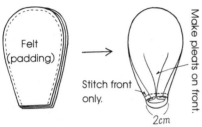

Felt (padding)

Stitch front only.

Make pleats on front.

2cm

③ With right sides facing and ears in between, sew head pieces together leaving bottom open. Turn to right side and stuff with fiberfill. Make body as for head.

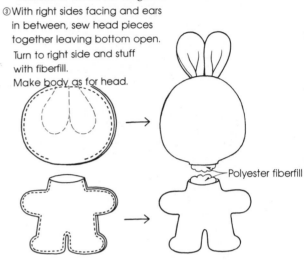

Polyester fiberfill

④ Match openings of head and body, turn in seam allowances and overcast.

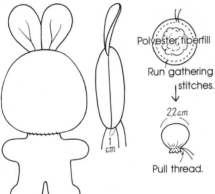

Rabbit

23 cm

Sew on beads.

Sew on nose.

2cm

⑤ Make nose.

Polyester fiberfill

Run gathering stitches.

2.2cm

1 cm

Pull thread.

⑥ Make dress.

Cut out 2 pieces each, adding 0.5cm for seam allowance.

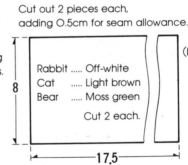

Rabbit ..... Off-white	
Cat ..... Light brown	
Bear ..... Moss green	
Cut 2 each.	

8

17.5

(c) Turn in seam allowance and machine-stitch.

0.5cm

Elastic tape

(b) Machine-stitch around armhole.

4.5 cm

(a) Sew side seams leaving 4.5cm open for armhole.

(d) Sew 17cm-long elastic tape along top edge.

(e) Fold hem and machine-stitch.

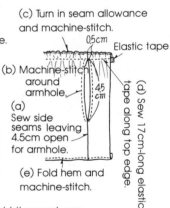

Make Cat and Bear as for Rabbit except ears.

For ears of Cat and Bear, sew pieces together with right sides facing. Turn to right side. Sew on in place.

2.5cm

23 cm

2.5cm

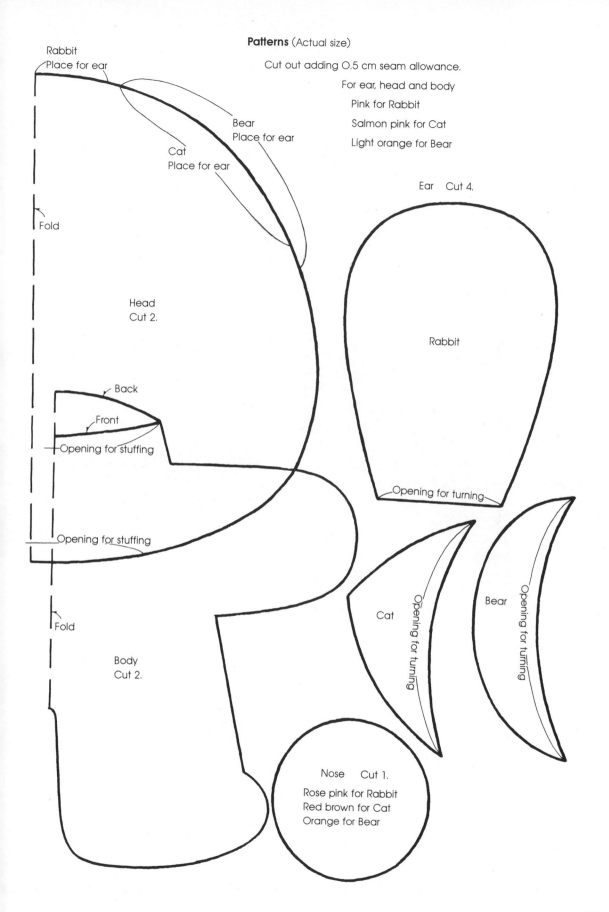

Patterns (Actual size)

Cut out adding 0.5 cm seam allowance.

For ear, head and body

Pink for Rabbit

Salmon pink for Cat

Light orange for Bear

Rabbit
Place for ear

Bear
Place for ear

Cat
Place for ear

Fold

Head
Cut 2.

Ear   Cut 4.

Rabbit

Back

Front

Opening for stuffing

Opening for stuffing

Opening for turning

Cat

Bear

Opening for turning

Opening for turning

Fold

Body
Cut 2.

Nose   Cut 1.

Rose pink for Rabbit
Red brown for Cat
Orange for Bear

5:BEDROOM

Bedspread
Instructions on page 70.

Bedspread, *shown on pages 68 & 69.*

MATERIALS:

Sheeting: Unbleached, 90cm by 750cm and moss green, 90cm by 350cm. Six-strand embroidery floss No. 25: 3 skeins each of bright yellow, red, orange, cobalt blue, brown, olive green and charcoal gray.

FINISHED SIZE: 146.5cm by 256.5cm

DIRECTIONS:

① Embroider on each piece in running stitch with colors indicated on next page. (about 4 stitches per 3cm)

② Piece embroidered squares following placement diagram. Join two pieces for lining together.

③ With wrong sides facing, bind edges of pieced top and lining together with moss-green border strips; sew border strips at top and bottom first and then each side.

Cutting Diagram

Add 1cm all around for seam allowance

Motif

Cut 23 pieces from unbleached sheeting and 22 from moss green.

27.5 × 27.5

Border   Cut 2 each.

9

Moss green

a = 137.5
b = 256.5

Join strips to make 137.5cm for (a) and 256.5cm for (b).

Piecing diagram

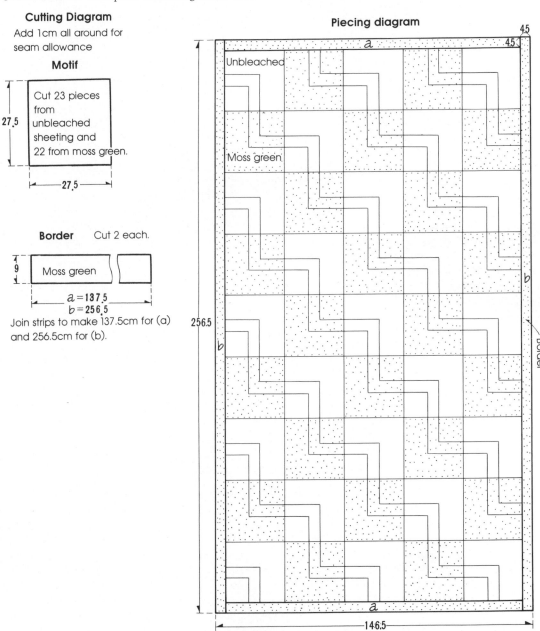

Cut lining 90cm by 249.5cm and 51.5cm by 249.5cm from unbleached sheeting.
Join pieces together with 1cm seam.

Color Key

Use 6 strands of floss.

	Moss green	Unbleached
(a)	Charcoal gray	Orange
(b)	Olive green	Bright yellow
(c)	Brown	Red
(d)	Cobalt blue	Cobalt blue
(e)	Red	Brown
(f)	Bright yellow	Olive green
(g)	Orange	Charcoal gray

Embroidery Pattern

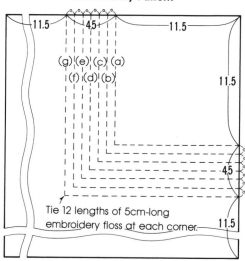

11.5   4.5   11.5

(g) (e) (c) (a)
(f) (d) (b)

11.5

4.5

11.5

Tie 12 lengths of 5cm-long embroidery floss at each corner.

Small Pillows
Instructions on page 74.

Ⓒ

Ⓔ

Ⓓ

Small Pillows, *shown on pages 72 & 73.*

MATERIALS:

Cotton broadcloth: See the list below for colors and amounts. Fabric for backing, 32cm square each. Pearl cotton # 5 in lavender for A. Sewing thread # 20 in light pink for B, C and E. Pearl cotton # 5 in wine red for D. For each: Quilt batting, 32cm square. Inner pillow, 32cm square. 30cm-long zipper.

FINISHED SIZE: 30cm square.

DIRECTIONS:

For A and D:

① Place quilt batting between top and backing. Quilt in running stitch as indicated.

② Sew zipper onto back pieces. With right sides facing, sew front and back together. Turn to right side and insert inner pillow.

For B, C and E:

① Cut out pieces as indicated. Sew pieces together following diagrams. Place quilt batting between pieced top and backing and quilt along seams.

② Make up for pillow as for A and D.

Diagram

Add 0.7cm all around for seam allowance.

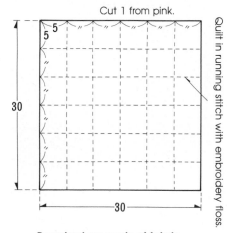

Front for A and D

Cut 1 from pink.

Quilt in running stitch with embroidery floss.

5, 5, 30, 30

Back (Same for A-E)

Use dull mauve for A, grayish wine red for D and pink for B, C and E.

30, Zipper, Seam allowance, 15, 15

Required amounts of fabric

	Fabric	Required amounts
A	Pink	32 cm square
	Dull mauve	36 cm × 32 cm
B	Pink	36 cm × 32 cm
	Light pink	90 cm × 8 cm
	Grayish wine red with floral design	68 cm × 8 cm
	Dull mauve	30 cm × 8 cm
C	Pink	36 cm × 32 cm
	Light pink	54 cm × 10 cm
	Grayish wine red with floral design	38 cm × 13 cm
	Grayish wine red	26 cm × 22 cm
D	Pink	32 cm square
	Grayish wine red	36 cm × 32 cm
E	Pink	36 cm × 32 cm
	Grayish wine red with floral design	52 cm × 13 cm
	Grayish wine red	52 cm × 8 cm
	Light pink	38 cm × 12 cm

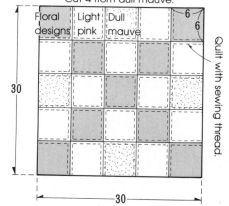

For B: Front

Cut 12 from light pink.
Cut 9 from floral designs.
Cut 4 from dull mauve.

Floral designs, Light pink, Dull mauve, 6, 6, 30, 30

Quilt with sewing thread.

For C: Front

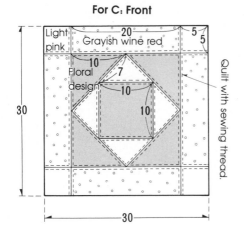

For E: Front

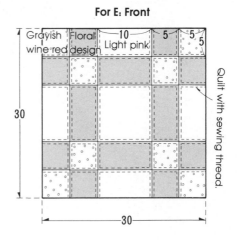

6:Bath & Toilette

Small Pictures, Tissue Box Covers and Sachets
Instructions for Pictures on page 78,
for Tissue Box Covers on page 104
and for Sachets on page 79.

Appliqué Patterns (Actual Size)

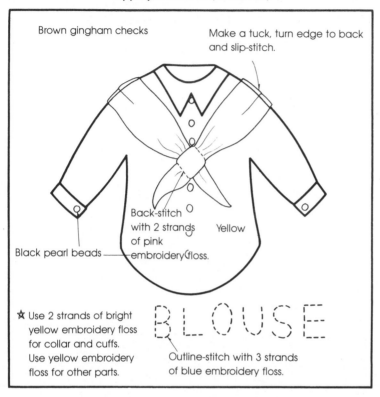

Brown gingham checks

Make a tuck, turn edge to back and slip-stitch.

Back-stitch with 2 strands of pink embroidery floss.

Yellow

Black pearl beads

★ Use 2 strands of bright yellow embroidery floss for collar and cuffs. Use yellow embroidery floss for other parts.

Outline-stitch with 3 strands of blue embroidery floss.

BLOUSE

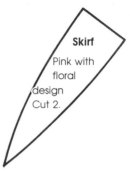

Skirt
Pink with floral design
Cut 2.

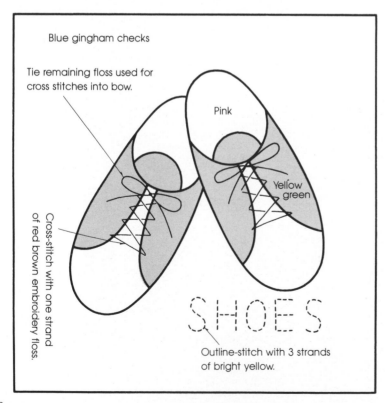

Blue gingham checks

Tie remaining floss used for cross stitches into bow.

Pink

Yellow green

Cross-stitch with one strand of red brown embroidery floss.

Outline-stitch with 3 strands of bright yellow.

SHOES

MATERIALS:

For Blouse Picture: Brown gingham checks, 10cm square. Cotton broadcloth: Scraps of yellow, and pink with floral design. Six-strand embroidery floss No. 25 in blue, pink, bright yellow and yellow. Iron-on interfacing, 18cm by 10cm. 9 black pearl beads. For Shoes Picture: Blue gingham checks, 10cm square. Scraps of pink and yellow green cotton broadcloth. Six-strand embroidery floss No. 25 in bright yellow, yellow green and pink. Pearl cotton # 5 in red brown. Iron-on interfacing, 20cm by 10cm. For each: Frame, 9cm square (inside measurements).

FINISHED SIZE: Same size as frame.

DIRECTIONS:

① Press iron-on interfacing on fabric for appliqué and cut out pieces using appliqué patterns. Press iron-on interfacing on gingham checks.

② Appliqué pieces in place using slip stitch. Embroider as indicated. Mount and frame.

Sachets, shown on pages 76 & 77.

MATERIALS:

For Sachet with Green Ribbon: Cotton broadcloth, beige with emerald green flowers, 9.5cm by 14cm. Emerald green satin ribbon, 0.6cm wide and 75cm long. Powder green cotton lace edging, 2.5cm by 38cm. Pink pearl bead, 0.6cm in diameter. For Sachet with Lavender Ribbon: Cotton broadcloth, beige with blue flowers, 6.5cm by 14cm. Lavender satin ribbon, 0.6cm by 62cm. Lavender cotton lace edging, 2.5cm by 28cm. 5 blue pearl beads, 0.3cm in diameter. For each: Potpourri.

FINISHED SIZE: See diagrams.

DIRECTIONS:

For Sachet with Green Ribbon:

① Place ribbon on broadcloth diagonally and machine-stitch along both edges.

② Sew lace edging along top edges. Sew side seams then fold bottom as shown and sew each corner.

③ Insert potpourri into bag and pull thread to close. Sew on ribbon bow and bead.

For Sachet with Lavender Ribbon:

① Place ribbon vertically and machine-stitch. Fold in half and sew side seams with lace edging in between.

② Insert potpourri into bag and pull thread to close. Sew on ribbon bow and beads.

Cutting Diagram

Add 0.5cm all around for seam allowance.

Sachet with Green Ribbon

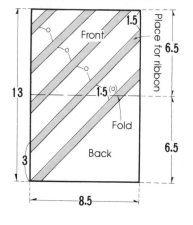

Sachet with Lavender Ribbon

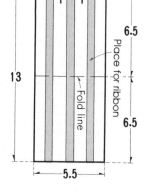

Finished Diagram

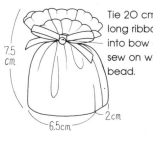

Tie 20 cm – long ribbon into bow and sew on with bead.

How to sew lace edging

2. Turn to right side and stitch.

1. With right sides of laces and fabric facing, sew together.

4. Run gathering stitches and insert potpourri. Pull thread to close.

3. Fold raw edges and stitch.

How to angle corner

Machine-stitch.

Side seam

Finished Diagram

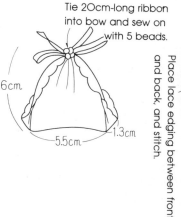

Tie 20cm-long ribbon into bow and sew on with 5 beads.

Details for Side and Top edge:

Lace edging (Right side)

Turn in top edge, run gathering stitches and insert potpourri. Pull thread to close.

Place lace edging between front and back, and stitch.

Bottom

Curtain with Valance
Instructions on page 81.

Paper Holder
Instructions on page 82.

Knob Covers
Instructions on page 82.

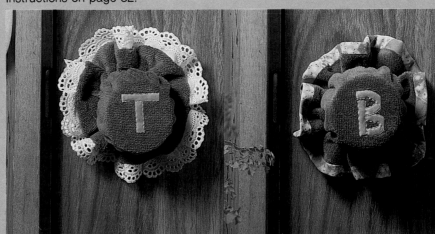

Curtain with Valance, *shown on page 80.*

MATERIALS:

Cotton broadcloth: White with small flowers, 88cm by 194cm; dark and light blue with small flowers, 88cm by 73cm. White cotton lace edging, 2cm by 480cm. White bias tape, 1.2cm by 176cm. 14 pin-on hooks.

FINISHED SIZE: See diagram.

DIRECTIONS:

① Cut fabric as indicated. Note that one side of the curtain is 5cm shorter than the other side. Make side hems and sew lace edging onto bottom edge.

② Place blue print on white, fold top edges and machine-stitch. Make pleats as indicated and insert hooks into pleats on the back.

③ Sew 2 pieces for tieback together, with lace edging between long edges and with loop at middle of each end.

Cutting Diagram

Add 1cm all around for seam allowance.

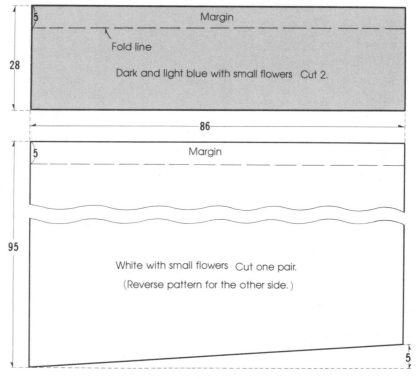

Margin

Fold line

Dark and light blue with small flowers Cut 2.

28

86

5

Margin

95

White with small flowers Cut one pair.

(Reverse pattern for the other side.)

5

Tieback

Dark and light blue with small flowers Cut 4 each. **Loop**

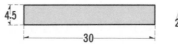

4.5

30

2 10

1cm

Fold in half lengthwise and machine-stitch.

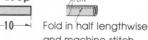

30cm

4.5cm 1cm

5cm

With wrong sides facing, turn in seam allowance, place lace edging and loops, and machine-stitch.

Finished Diagram

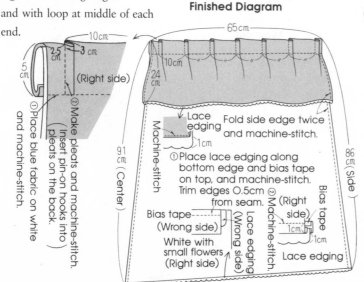

10cm

2.5 cm 3 cm

5 cm (Right side)

①Place blue fabric on white and machine-stitch.

②Make pleats and machine-stitch. (Insert pin-on hooks into pleats on the back.)

65cm

10cm

24 cm

91 cm (Center)

Machine-stitch

Lace edging

1cm

Fold side edge twice and machine-stitch.

①Place lace edging along bottom edge and bias tape on top, and machine-stitch. Trim edges 0.5cm ② from seam.

Bias tape (Wrong side)

Lace edging (Wrong side)

②Machine-stitch

White with small flowers (Right side)

(Right side)

1cm

1cm

Bias tape

86 cm (Side)

Lace edging

Paper Holder, *shown on page 80*

MATERIALS:

Blue terrycloth, 14.5cm by 61cm. Blue cotton broadcloth, 14.5cm by 6cm. White cotton lace edging, 2.5cm by 137cm. Sky blue satin ribbon, 0.6cm by 17cm. Blue bias tape, 1.2cm by 149cm.

FINISHED SIZE: See diagram.

DIRECTIONS:

① Cut fabric as indicated. Sew lace edging along three sides of terrycloth with bias tape.

② Fold one third from the bottom as shown and sew bias tape onto edge. Stitch top and bottom edges of broadcloth and slip-stitch in place.

③ Sew ribbon bow in place.

Cutting Diagram

Add 0.5cm all around to terrycloth and 1cm to broadcloth for seam allowance.

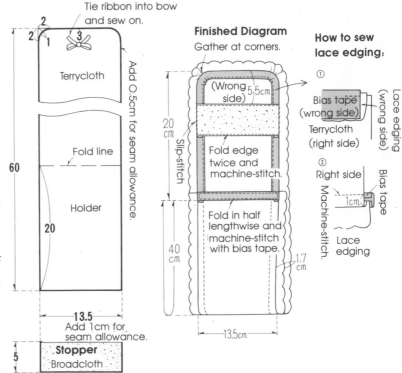

Knob Covers, *shown on page 80.*

MATERIALS:

For Knob Cover at left: Blue terrycloth, 22cm in diameter.

Sky blue satin ribbon, 0.6cm by 8cm. White cotton lace edging, 2.5cm by 80cm. Blue bias tape, 1.2cm by 117cm. Round elastic tape, 15cm. For Knob Cover at

Diagram

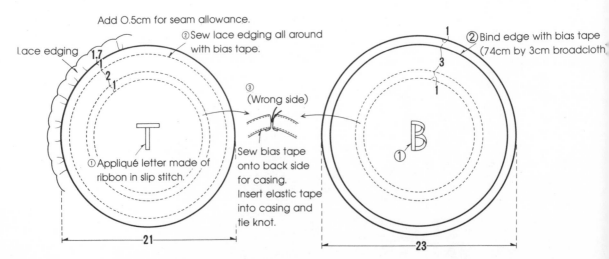

right: Blue terrycloth, 23cm in diameter. Dark and light blue with small flowers, 55cm square. Sky blue satin ribbon, 0.6cm by 15cm. Blue bias tape, 1.2cm by 50cm. Round elastic tape, 15cm.

FINISHED SIZE: See diagrams.

DIRECTIONS:

Cut out pieces as indicated. Make up for Knob Cover following instructions shown on opposite page.

Appliqué Patterns (Actual Size)
Use satin ribbon.
Turn in 0.5cm.

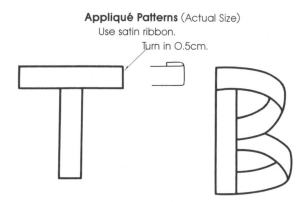

Pencil Case and Tissue Cases, *shown on pages 4 & 5.*

For Pencil Case:

MATERIALS:

Heavyweight cotton fabric: Cream, 18cm by 17cm; beige, 11cm by 5cm; pink, 9cm by 6cm. Six-strand embroidery floss No. 25 in cherry pink, yellow green and brown. 12cm-long zipper.

FINISHED SIZE: 7cm by 16.5cm.

DIRECTIONS:

Cut out pieces adding 0.7cm all around for seam allowance. Make up for Pencil Case following instructions below.

Cutting Diagram
Add 0.7cm all around for seam allowance.

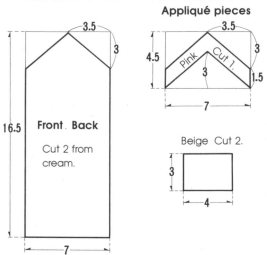

Appliqué pieces

3.5 · 3 · 4.5 · Pink · Cut 1. · 3 · 1.5 · 7

16.5 · **Front . Back** · Cut 2 from cream. · 7

Beige Cut 2.

3 · 4

Finished Diagram

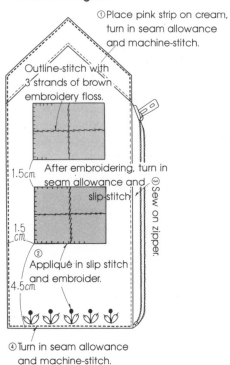

① Place pink strip on cream, turn in seam allowance and machine-stitch.

Outline-stitch with 3 strands of brown embroidery floss.

1.5cm

After embroidering, turn in seam allowance and slip-stitch.

③ Sew on zipper.

1.5 cm

②

4.5cm

Appliqué in slip stitch and embroider.

④ Turn in seam allowance and machine-stitch.

Embroidery Pattern (Actual Size)
French knot
Use 6 strands of cherry pink embroidery floss.

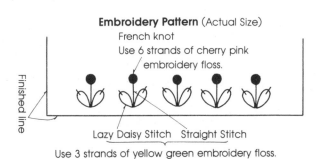

Finished line

Lazy Daisy Stitch   Straight Stitch
Use 3 strands of yellow green embroidery floss.

For Tissue Cases:

MATERIALS:

Heavyweight cotton: For Tissue Case with pink window: Cream, 14cm by 17cm; ivory, 14cm by 7cm; beige, 14cm by 7cm; pink, 10cm by 5cm. Six-strand embroidery floss No. 25 in wine red. For Tissue Case with beige window: Cream, 14cm by 17cm; ivory, 14cm by 7cm; pink, 14cm by 7cm; beige, 10cm by 5cm. Six-strand embroidery floss No. 25 in olive green.

FINISHED SIZE: 12cm by 9cm.

Cutting Diagram

Add 0.7cm all around for seam allowance unless otherwise indicated.

Front

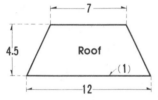

Cut 1 each from ivory and cream. Use same color for both cases.

4.5

(1)

Side for opening

12

Back

9

Cream for both cases

12

DIRECTIONS:

① Sew roof on ivory piece and window on cream piece.

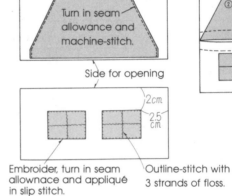

Turn in seam allowance and machine-stitch.

Side for opening

2cm

2.5 cm

Embroider, turn in seam allownace and appliqué in slip stitch.

Outline-stitch with 3 strands of floss.

③ With right sides facing, sew front and back together. Turn inside out.

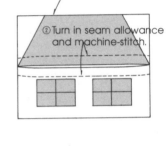

② Turn in seam allowance and machine-stitch.

Pieces for Appliqué

7

4.5

Roof

(1)

12

Beige for pink window case
Pink for beige window case } Cut 1.

Window

2.5

3.5

Pink for beige roof case
Beige for pink roof case } Cut 2

Continued from Page 15.

For E: Make up for pincushion following illustrated instructions at right.

E (Actual Size)

Cut out upper piece and appliqué adding 0.5 cm all around for seam allowance.

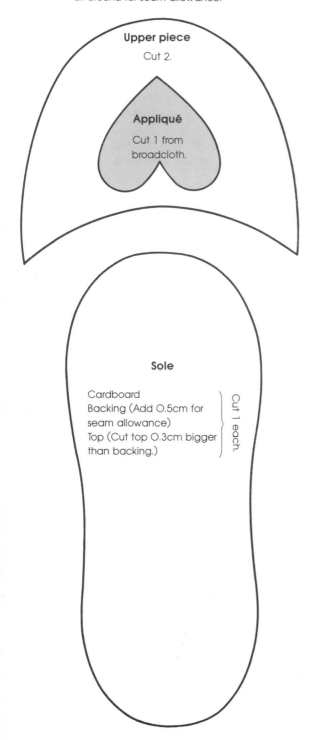

Upper piece

Cut 2.

Appliqué

Cut 1 from broadcloth.

Sole

Cardboard
Backing (Add 0.5cm for seam allowance)
Top (Cut top 0.3cm bigger than backing.)

Cut 1 each.

DIRECTIONS:

① Appliqué onto upper piece.

Turn in seam allowance, stuff thinly with fiberfill and slip-stitch.

② With right sides facing, sew pieces together. Turn to right side.

Clip into curves.

③ With right sides facing and upper piece in between, sew top and backing of sole together. Turn to right side.

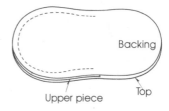

Backing

Top

Upper piece

④ Insert cardboard between top and backing, stuff with fiberfill, turn in seam allowance and slip-stitch.

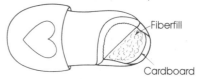

Fiberfill

Cardboard

Finished Diagram

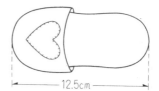

12.5cm

MATERIALS:

For Scissors at left: Light purple velveteen and cotton fabric for lining, 26cm by 29cm each. Purple cotton broadcloth with orange flowers, 40cm square. Six-strand embroidery floss No. 25 in light purple and purple. For Scissors Case at right: Purple velveteen and cotton fabric for lining, 26cm by 29cm each. Lavender cotton broadcloth with light orange flowers, 40cm square. Six-strand embroidery floss No. 25 in light purple. For each: Quilt batting, 26cm by 29cm.

FINISHED SIZE: See diagram.

DIRECTIONS:

Cut out pieces adding no seam allowance. Place top, batting and lining together and baste. Quilt along quilting lines. Make up for scissors case following instructions on next page.

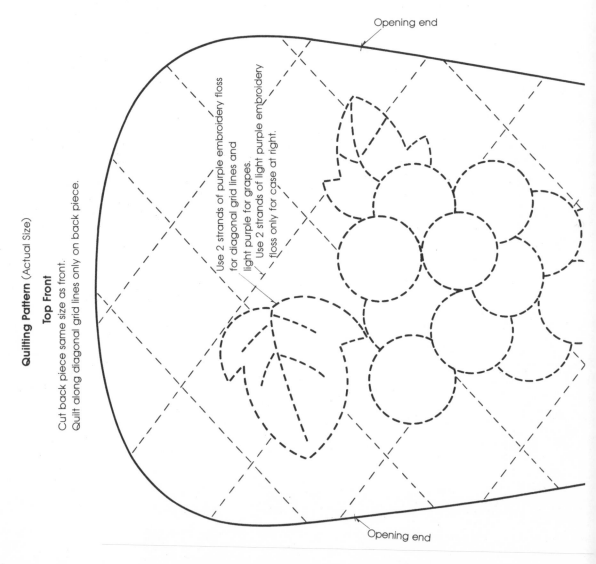

Quilting Pattern (Actual Size)

Top Front

Cut back piece same size as front.
Quilt along diagonal grid lines only on back piece.

Use 2 strands of purple embroidery floss for diagonal grid lines and light purple for grapes.

Use 2 strands of light purple embroidery floss only for case at right.

Opening end

Opening end

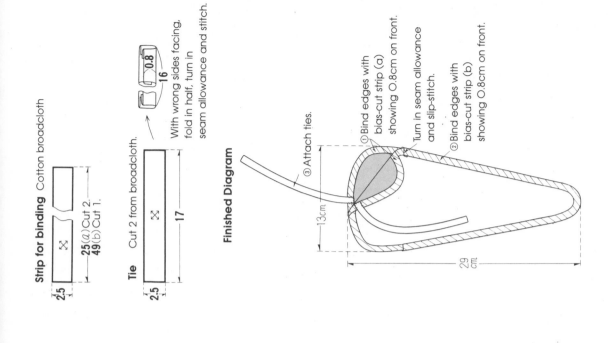

Strip for binding Cotton broadcloth

X

2.5

25 (a) Cut 2.
49 (b) Cut 1.

Tie Cut 2 from broadcloth.

X

2.5

17

0.8

16

With wrong sides facing,
fold in half, turn in
seam allowance and stitch.

Finished Diagram

① Bind edges with
bias-cut strip (a)
showing 0.8cm on front.

Turn in seam allowance
and slip-stitch.

② Bind edges with
bias-cut strip (b)
showing 0.8cm on front.

③ Attach ties.

13cm

29 cm

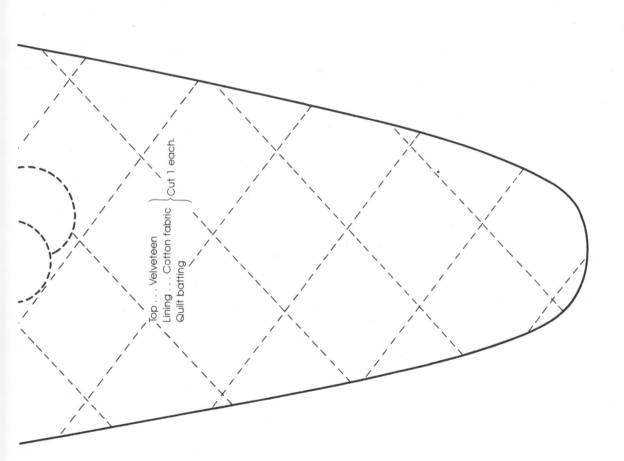

Top . . . Velveteen
Lining . . . Cotton fabric } Cut 1 each.
Quilt batting

Pochettes, *shown on page 20.*

MATERIALS:

For Ivory Pochette: Unbleached canvas, 45cm square. Felt: Blue, 8cm by 5cm and scrap of navy. Six-strand embroidery floss No. 25 in navy, ivory and blue. White cotton cord, 0.5cm in diameter and 120cm long. For Red Pochette: Red terrycloth, 45cm square. Felt: Pink, 8cm by 5cm and scrap of navy. Six-strand embroidery floss No. 25 in navy, red and pink. Red cotton cord, 0.5cm in diameter and 120cm long. For each: 17cm long zipper. 2 plastic rings, 1.7cm in inner diameter.

FINISHED SIZE: See diagram.

DIRECTIONS:

Cut out pieces. Appliqué onto front in slip stitch and embroider. Make up for pochette following instructions below.

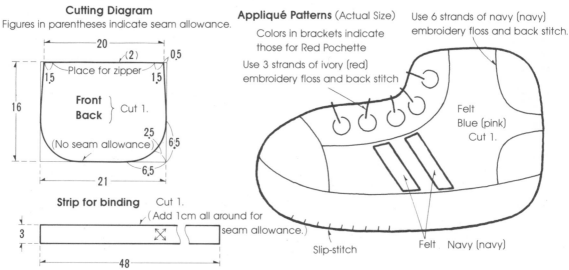

Cutting Diagram
Figures in parentheses indicate seam allowance.

20
(2)   0.5
Place for zipper
1.5   1.5

Front
Back } Cut 1.

16

2.5
(No seam allowance)   6.5
6.5
21

Strip for binding   Cut 1.
(Add 1cm all around for seam allowance.)
3
48

Appliqué Patterns (Actual Size)
Colors in brackets indicate those for Red Pochette
Use 3 strands of ivory (red) embroidery floss and back stitch

Use 6 strands of navy (navy) embroidery floss and back stitch.

Felt
Blue (pink)
Cut 1.

Slip-stitch
Felt   Navy (navy)

Finished Diagram

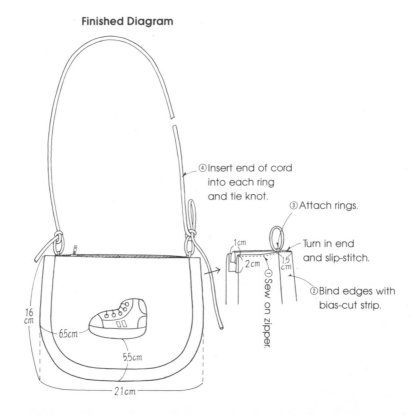

④Insert end of cord into each ring and tie knot.

③Attach rings.

Turn in end and slip-stitch.

1cm
2cm
1.5 cm

①Sew on zipper.

②Bind edges with bias-cut strip.

16 cm
6.5cm
5.5cm
21cm

Shoe Cases, *shown on page 21.*

MATERIALS:

For Orange Shoe Case: Cotton broadcloth: Orange, and white with orange leaf design, 32cm by 25cm each. Brown sheeting for lining, 32cm by 47cm. Felt for appliqué: Brown, 10cm by 4cm and scrap of white. Six-strand embroidery floss No. 25 in beige, brown and white. 30cm-long dark brown zipper. 10 beige buttons, 1.1cm in diameter. For Blue Shoe Case: Cotton broadcloth: Sky blue, and white with gray leaf design, 32cm by 25cm each. Blue sheeting for lining, 32cm by 47cm. Felt for appliqué: Gray, 10cm by 4cm and scrap of white. Six-strand embroidery floss No. 25 in cream, gray and white. 30cm-long gray zipper. 10 gray buttons, 1.1cm in diameter.

FINISHED SIZE: See diagram.

DIRECTIONS:

① Cut out pieces adding 1cm for seam allowance.

② Sew zipper in place and appliqué. Sew on buttons.

③ With right sides facing, sew center back seam.

④ Fold corner as shown and stitch to make side. Turn to right side.

⑤ Sew pieces for lining in same manner and insert into outer case. Slip-stitch top-edges onto wrong side.

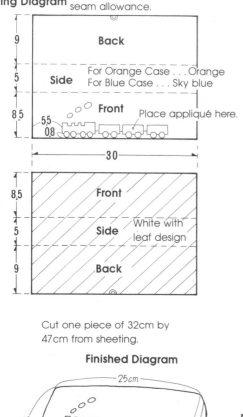

Cutting Diagram Add 1cm all around for seam allowance.

9

5

8.5

5.5

0.8

Back

Side — For Orange Case...Orange / For Blue Case...Sky blue

Front — Place appliqué here.

—30—

8.5

5

9

Front

Side — White with leaf design

Back

Cut one piece of 32cm by 47cm from sheeting.

Finished Diagram

—25cm—

18 cm

1cm — Zipper

5 cm

Sew outer and inner cases together at each corner.

Detail for Side

Side seam

5cm

1cm

Stitch.

Cut off shaded area.

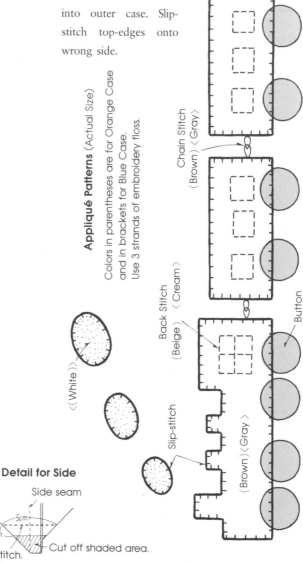

Appliqué Patterns (Actual Size)

Colors in parentheses are for Orange Case and in brackets for Blue Case. Use 3 strands of embroidery floss.

Chain Stitch (Brown) ⟨Gray⟩

Back Stitch (Beige) ⟨Cream⟩

Button

⟨White⟩

Slip-stitch

(Brown) ⟨Gray⟩

Continued from page 19.

Picture at right.

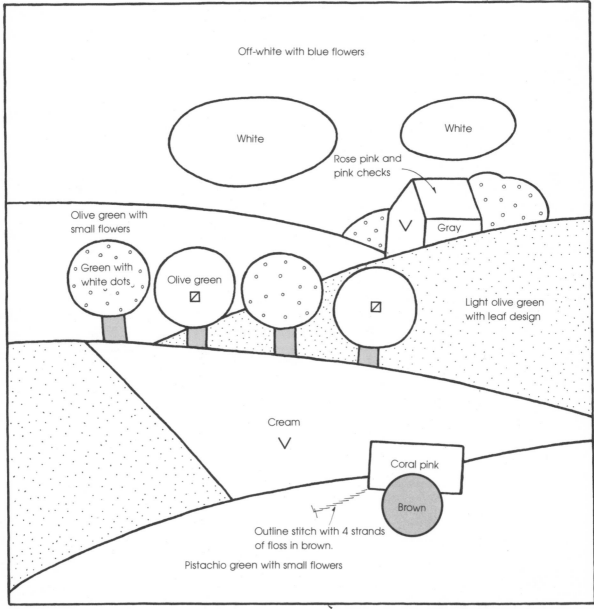

Off-white with blue flowers

White

White

Rose pink and
pink checks

Gray

Olive green with
small flowers

Green with
white dots

Olive green

Light olive green
with leaf design

Cream

V

Coral pink

Brown

Outline stitch with 4 strands
of floss in brown.

Pistachio green with small flowers

Add 3cm for margin to pieces which are placed at
side.

Continued from page 31.

Diagram

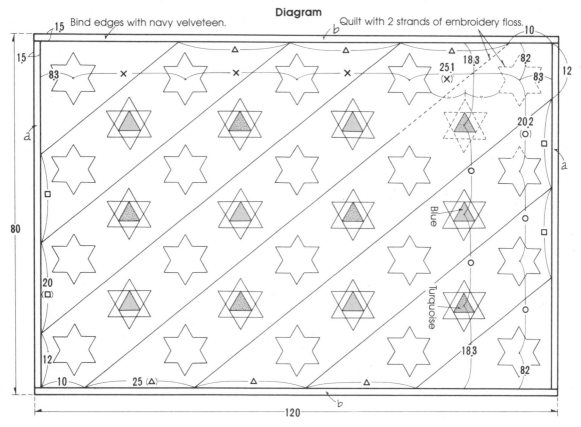

Bind edges with navy velveteen.

Quilt with 2 strands of embroidery floss.

Cut one piece 80cm by 120cm from navy velveteen for background.

How to inset triangles:

② Place inset pieces under cut-out area, turn in seam allowance of navy velveteen and slip-stitch.

① Cut out 3cm-triangles from indicated stars. Slip into points.

Strip for binding

Add 1cm for seam allowance.

Navy velveteen Cut 2 each.	

a = 77
b = 120

Mat, *shown on page 37.*

MATERIALS:

Cotton broadcloth: Yellow green, 84cm by 32cm; unbleached with lavender design, 42cm by 26cm; unbleached with pink design, 25cm by 15cm. Pink sheeting, 48cm by 17cm. Six-strand embroidery floss No. 25 in yellow green, lavender, pink and matching colors with cotton broadcloth. Iron-on interfacing, 42cm by 32cm. Polyester fiberfill.

FINISHED SIZE: 40cm by 30cm.

Cutting Diagram

Add 1cm for seam allowance.

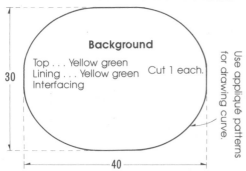

Background

Top . . . Yellow green
Lining . . . Yellow green   Cut 1 each.
Interfacing

Use appliqué patterns for drawing curve.

30

40

DIRECTIONS:

① Press iron-on interfacing on wrong side of top piece.

② Appliqué and embroider on top.

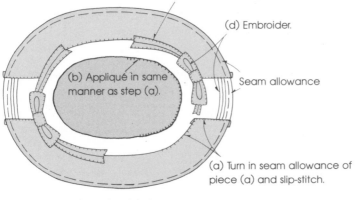

(c) Appliqué in same manner as step (a), but stuff thinly with fiberfill.

(d) Embroider.

(b) Appliqué in same manner as step (a).

Seam allowance

(a) Turn in seam allowance of piece (a) and slip-stitch.

③ With right sides facing, turn in seam allowance and slip-stitch.

Fold

Fold

Center

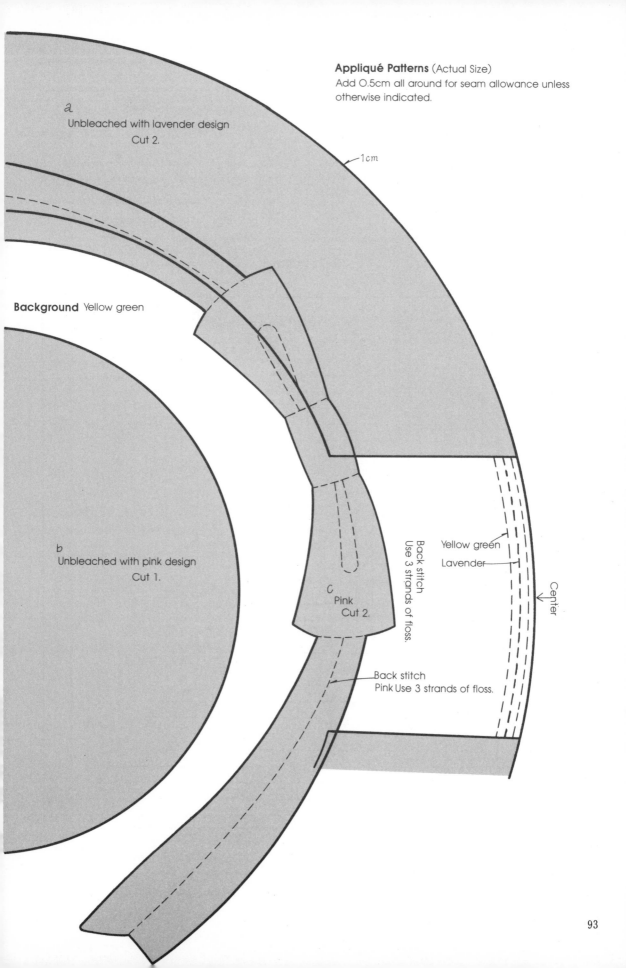

Appliqué Patterns (Actual Size)
Add 0.5cm all around for seam allowance unless otherwise indicated.

1cm

a
Unbleached with lavender design
Cut 2.

Background Yellow green

b
Unbleached with pink design
Cut 1.

c
Pink
Cut 2.

Back stitch
Use 3 strands of floss.

Yellow green

Lavender

Center

Back stitch
Pink Use 3 strands of floss.

Dishcloths, shown on page 41.

MATERIALS:

Sheeting, 67cm by 35cm each of green, umber and unbleached. Heavy-duty sewing thread in navy and white for Green cloth, red for Umber cloth and navy for Unbleached cloth.

FINISHED SIZE: 32.5cm square.

DIRECTIONS:

① Fold fabric in half with right sides facing. Stitch three sides leaving opening for turning. Turn to right side and slip-stitch opening closed.

② Transfer design to fabric matching centers.

③ Use 2 strands of thread in needle for Green and Umber cloths and 1 strand for Unbleached cloth. Make a knot at end of thread, insert needle into fabric and pull thread until the knot enters between front and back pieces. Then start stitching.

Green Dishcloth

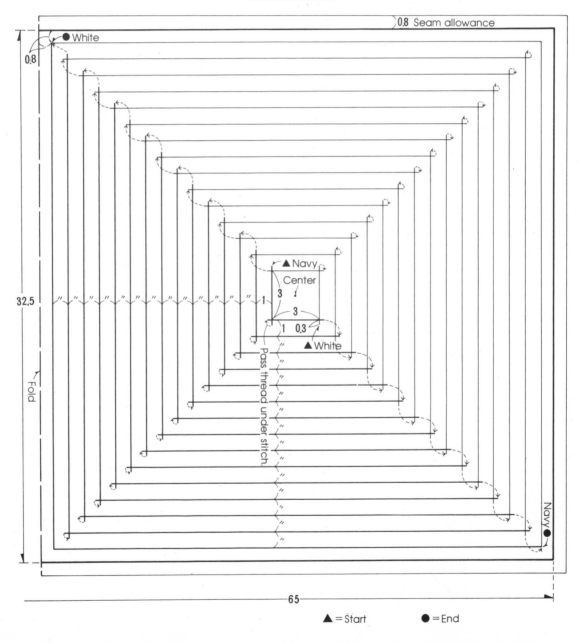

▲ = Start   ● = End

Umber Dishcloth

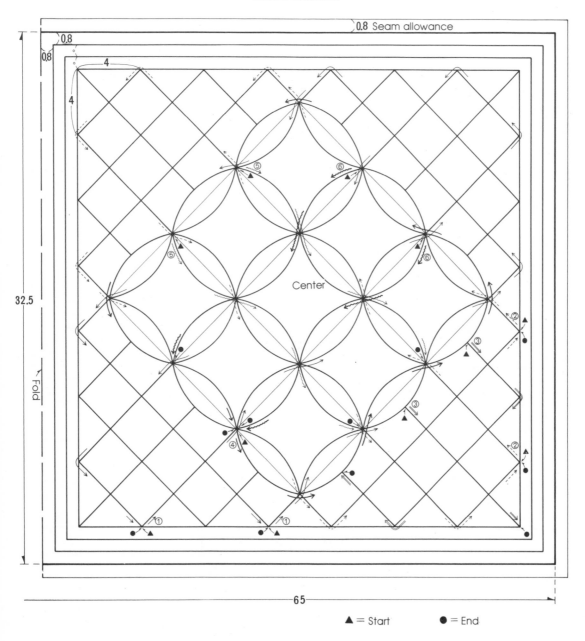

0.8 Seam allowance

0.8

0.8

4

4

32.5

Fold

Center

65

▲ = Start   ● = End

Unbleached Dishcloth

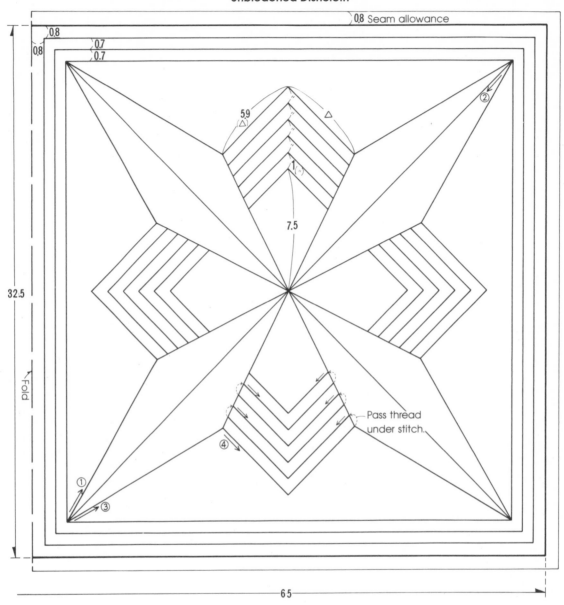

0.8 Seam allowance

0.8

0.8

0.7

0.7

②

5.9
(△)

△

1

7.5

Pass thread
under stitch.

④

①

③

32.5

Fold

6 5

Curtain, shown on page 44.

MATERIALS:

Cotton broadcloth, blue with white flowers, 90cm by 144cm. White cotton lace edging, 5.5cm by 220cm. 14 plastic rings, 1.5cm in inner diameter. White bias tape, 1.2cm by 174cm.

FINISHED SIZE: See diagram.

DIRECTIONS:

Cut fabric and make up for curtain following instructions on next page.

Cutting Diagram

Figures in parentheses indicate seam allowance.

(5)

(15)

66

Cut 2.

Fold

(1)

87

Finished Diagram

③ Sew on ring.

② Stitch top and side hems.

1 cm

70.5 cm

4cm

(Wrong side)

1cm

87cm

4.5cm

① Sew on lace edging.

Make pleats.

Bias tape

(Wrong side)

(Wrong side)

Right side

Lace edging

Slip-stitch.

Fold edges twice and machine-stitch.

Seam allowance

With right sides of broadcloth and bias tape facing and lace in between, stitch, making pleats on lace as you sew.

Lunch Bags, shown on page 45.

MATERIALS:

For top piece: Navy gingham checks, blue cotton broadcloth with animal design and pink with animal design, 90cm by 45cm each. For lining: Cotton broadcloth: Navy, blue and pink, 90cm by 35cm each. Flannel, 22cm by 17cm. Bias tape: Navy, blue and pink 1.2cm by 241cm.

FINISHED SIZE: See diagram.

DIRECTIONS:

Cut out pieces and make up for lunch bag following instructions on next page.

Cutting Diagram

Add 1cm for seam allowance unless otherwise indicated.

Figures in parentheses indicate seam allowance.

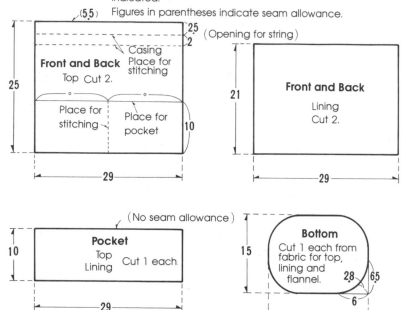

(5.5)

.25

2

(Opening for string)

Casing

Front and Back

Top Cut 2.

Place for stitching

25

Place for stitching

Place for pocket

10

29

21

Front and Back

Lining Cut 2.

29

(No seam allowance)

Pocket

Top

Lining

Cut 1 each.

10

29

15

Bottom

Cut 1 each from fabric for top, lining and flannel.

28

6.5

6

20

Finished Diagram

Turn in end 0.5cm and take a stitch at each side.

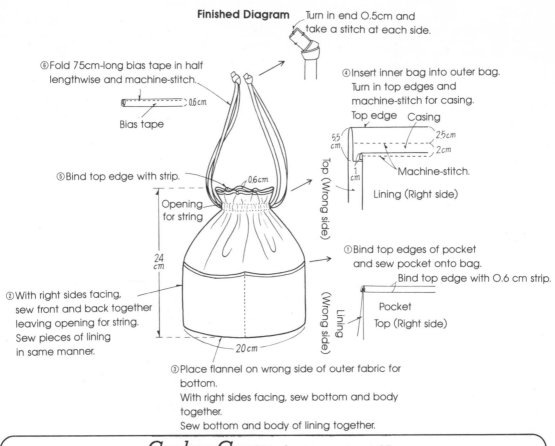

⑥Fold 75cm-long bias tape in half lengthwise and machine-stitch.

0.6cm

Bias tape

④Insert inner bag into outer bag. Turn in top edges and machine-stitch for casing.

Top edge   Casing

5.5 cm

25cm

2cm

1 cm

Machine-stitch.

Lining (Right side)

Top (Wrong side)

⑤Bind top edge with strip.

0.6cm

Opening for string

①Bind top edges of pocket and sew pocket onto bag.

Bind top edge with 0.6 cm strip.

Pocket

Top (Right side)

24 cm

②With right sides facing, sew front and back together leaving opening for string. Sew pieces of lining in same manner.

Lining (Wrong side)

20cm

③Place flannel on wrong side of outer fabric for bottom.
With right sides facing, sew bottom and body together.
Sew bottom and body of lining together.

Cooker Cover, *shown on page 45.*

MATERIALS:

Cotton fabric: Yellow green with heart design and yellow-green gingham checks, 50cm square each. White cotton broadcloth with yellow-green dots, 35cm square. Green bias tape, 1.8cm by 275cm. Self-covered button, 2.5cm in diameter.

FINISHED SIZE: 50cm in diameter.

Diagram

Top ----- Yellow green with heart design
Lining --- Gingham checks

Cut 1 each.

Inner circle
White with yellow-green dots
Cut 1.

Sew on self-covered button.

0.8

Bias tape

DIRECTIONS:

①Cut out inner and outer circles.
②Bind edge of inner circle. Sew inner circle to outer circle.

Inner Circle (Right side)

0.8cm

Bias tape

0.8cm

Bias tape

Top (Right side)

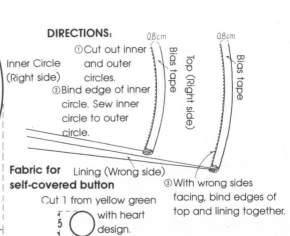

Fabric for self-covered button

Cut 1 from yellow green with heart design.

5

Lining (Wrong side)

③With wrong sides facing, bind edges of top and lining together.

35
50

Napkins, *shown on page 45.*

MATERIALS:

Cotton broadcloth: For pink Napkin: Pink with white flowers, 44cm square; light pink, 26cm square; dark pink, 15cm square. For Blue Napkin: White with blue flowers, 44cm square; light blue, 26cm square; dark blue, 15cm square.

FINISHED SIZE: 40cm square.

DIRECTIONS:

① Cut out appliqué pieces adding 0.5cm for seam allowance. Appliqué onto corner of napkin.

② Fold edges twice and machine-stitch except appliquéd corner. Slip-stitch edges of appliquéd corner.

Diagram

Add 2cm all around for seam allowance unless otherwise indicated.

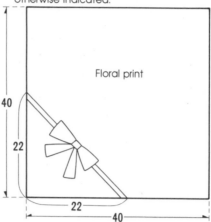

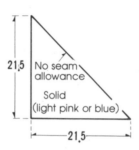

Appliqué Pattern (Actual Size)

Add 0.5cm all around for seam allowance.

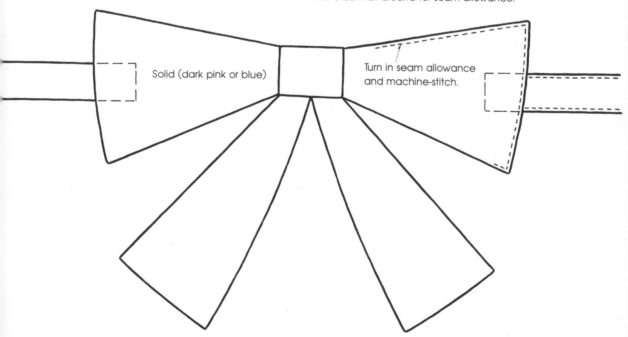

Wall Hanging with Big Pocket, *shown on page 53.*

MATERIALS:

Cotton broadcloth: Navy, 55cm by 46cm; blue, 52cm by 32cm; lavender, 30cm by 14cm; red brown and sky blue with flowers, 10cm by 13cm each; purple, 7cm by 9cm; bluish purple with elephant design, 18cm by 14cm. Navy denim, 36cm by 46cm. White cotton lace edging, 1.3cm by 37cm. Elastic tape, 0.6cm by 35cm. Quilt batting, 36cm by 46cm.

FINISHED SIZE: See diagram.

DIRECTIONS:

① Cut out pieces.

② Baste top, batting and lining for background together and quilt.

③ Sew on small pocket.

④ Sew pieces of big pocket together. Sew on pocket. Make casing at top edge and insert elastic tape.

⑤ Gather bottom edge of big pocket. Place pocket on background and bind edges with navy strip.

⑥ Sew on loops for dowel.

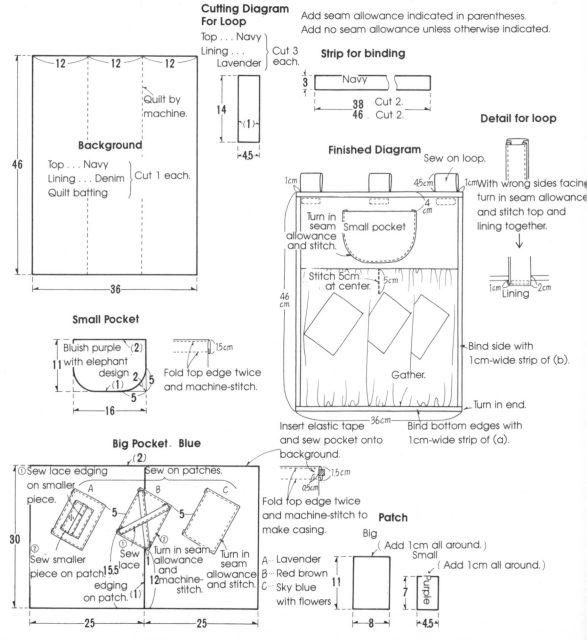

Add seam allowance indicated in parentheses.
Add no seam·allowance unless otherwise indicated.

Continued from page 55.

Embroidery and Appliqué Patterns (Actual Size) Add 0.5cm all around to appliqué pieces for seam allowance.
Use 2 strands of embroidery floss.

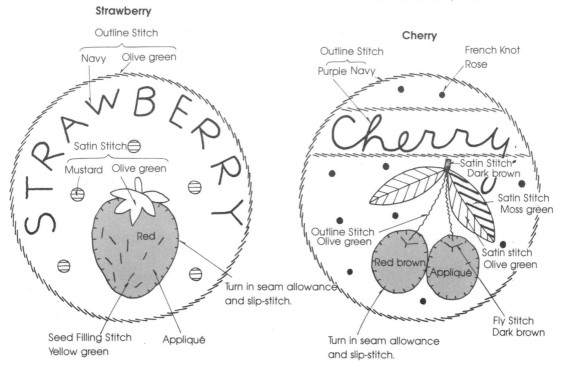

Strawberry

Outline Stitch
Navy   Olive green

Satin Stitch
Mustard   Olive green

Red

Turn in seam allowance and slip-stitch.

Seed Filling Stitch
Yellow green

Appliqué

Cherry

Outline Stitch
Purple Navy

French Knot
Rose

Satin Stitch
Dark brown

Satin Stitch
Moss green

Outline Stitch
Olive green

Satin stitch
Olive green

Red brown   Appliqué

Turn in seam allowance and slip-stitch.

Fly Stitch
Dark brown

Blackberry

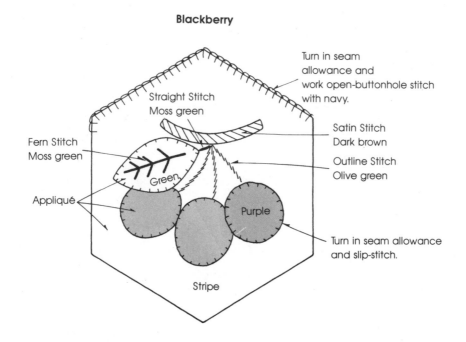

Straight Stitch
Moss green

Turn in seam allowance and work open-buttonhole stitch with navy.

Satin Stitch
Dark brown

Fern Stitch
Moss green

Outline Stitch
Olive green

Green

Appliqué

Purple

Turn in seam allowance and slip-stitch.

Stripe

101

Smock Wall Hanging with Pockets, *shown on page 56.*

MATERIALS:

Light brown checked heavyweight cotton fabric and dull mauve sheeting, **53cm** by 42cm each. Sheeting: Beige, 15cm by 36cm and blue gray, 11cm by 12cm. Sage green canvas, 11cm by 12cm. Scraps of cotton broadcloth in following colors: Rose pink, brown checks, beige with flowers, old rose and cream. Scrap of white with dark and light green checked cotton fabric. Six-strand embroidery floss No. 25 in old rose. Light brown bias tape, 1.2cm by 50cm.

FINISHED SIZE: See diagram.

Cutting Diagram

Add seam allowance indicated in parentheses.

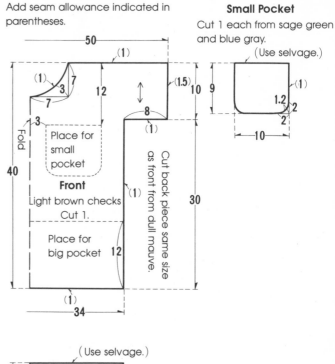

Small Pocket

Cut 1 each from sage green and blue gray.

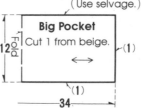

Appliqué Patterns (Actual Size)

For Left Pocket

Old rose

Beige with flowers

Brown checks

Rose pink

Slip-stitch.

For Right Pocket

White with dark and light green checks

Cream

Slip-stitch.

DIRECTIONS:

①Sew bias tape along neck edge. Machine-stitch.

②Fold sleeve edge and machine-stitch.

③Appliqué onto small pockets seam allowance. and sew them onto front.

Sew opening edge same manner as sleeve edge.

④ Sew big pocket onto front.

⑤With right sides facing, sew front and back together except neck and sleeve edges. Turn to right side and top-stitch along shoulders, underarms and bottom edges.

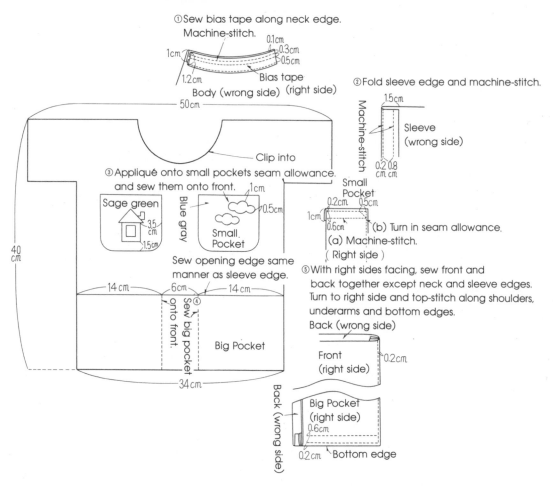

0.1cm
0.3cm
0.5cm
1cm
1.2cm
Bias tape
Body (wrong side) (right side)

1.5cm
Machine-stitch
Sleeve (wrong side)
0.2 0.8 cm cm

50cm
Clip into

Sage green
Blue gray
3.5 cm
1.5cm
Small Pocket
1cm
0.5cm

Small Pocket
0.2cm 0.5cm
1cm
0.6cm
(b) Turn in seam allowance.
(a) Machine-stitch.
(Right side)

40 cm

14cm 6cm 14cm
Big Pocket
34cm
Back (wrong side)

Back (wrong side)
Front (right side)
0.2cm

Big Pocket (right side)
0.6cm
0.2cm Bottom edge

MATERIALS:

For Cover at left: Off-white cotton broadcloth with orange flowers, 88cm by 13cm. Orange gingham checks, 54cm by 7cm. Light brown satin ribbon, 0.6cm by 350cm. Beige cotton lace edging, 3cm by 182cm. Orange hem tape, 1.2cm by 84cm. Iron-on interfacing, 88cm by 18cm. For Cover at right: Off-white cotton broadcloth with pink flowers, 88cm by 13cm. Pink gingham checks, 42cm by 10cm. Pink satin ribbon, 0.6cm by 330cm. Pink cotton lace edging, 3cm by 250cm. Pink hem tape, 1.2cm by 30cm. 4 pink pearl beads, 0.5 cm in diameter. Iron-on interfacing, 88cm by 26cm.

FINISHED SIZE: See diagram.

DIRECTIONS:

For Cover at left:

①Sew on ribbon as indicated.

②Sew on lace edging and border following illustration on next page.

③Press iron-on interfacing on wrong side of top piece.

④With right sides facing, sew center seam leaving 16cm open.

⑤Fold bottom edge, place tape on and machine-stitch.

⑥Join side edges together as shown on next page. Sew on ribbon bows in place.

For Cover at right:

①Sew on ribbon as indicated.

②Sew on lace and border following illustration. Press iron-on interfacing on border.

③With right sides facing, sew center seam leaving 16cm open.

④Sew pocket on one side. Fold bottom edge and sew on tape.

⑤Join side edges together as for Cover at left. Sew ribbon onto pocket and beads in place.

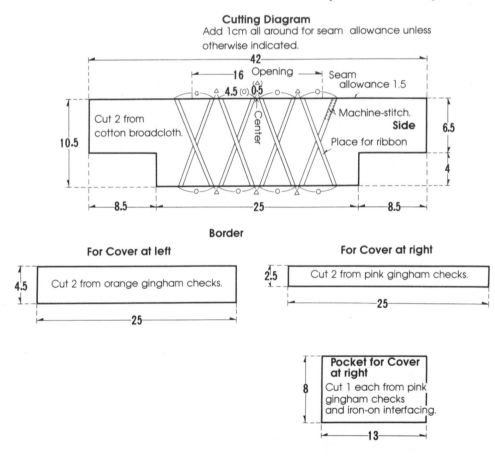

Cutting Diagram
Add 1cm all around for seam allowance unless otherwise indicated.

Border

For Cover at left

Cut 2 from orange gingham checks.

For Cover at right

Cut 2 from pink gingham checks.

Pocket for Cover at right
Cut 1 each from pink gingham checks and iron-on interfacing.

Finished Diagram for Cover at left

Detail for Center Opening

Lace edging (right side)

Ribbon

1.5 cm

Seam

End of stitching

Top-stitch.

Opening

Tie 17cm-long ribbon into bow and sew on.

13cm 1.5cm 25cm 1.5cm

ⓑ

Opening

8.5 cm ⓐ

4.5cm

1.5cm

2 cm 2 cm

Detail for corner

Side (Right side)

1cm

Machine-stitch twice.

Iron-on interfacing

Cut off.

0.5 cm

How to sew on lace edging

ⓐ

Side (right side)
Gather 34cm-long lace edging.

1cm

1cm 1.5cm (Right side)

Border (Right side)

Sew side and border pieces together with gathered lace in between.

ⓑ

1.5cm

Seam allowance for opening

1cm

0.4 cm

Ribbon (right side)

Right
2cm side

Gather 57cm-long lace edging.

(Right side)

Sew on gathered lace edging placing ribbon on top.

Detail for bottom edge

Iron-on interfacing

Machine-stitch.

Tape (right side)

1 cm

0.2 cm

Finished Diagram for Cover at right

13cm 25cm 0.5cm

ⓑ 1.5 cm 0.5 cm Opening

8.5 cm ⓐ

Tie 17cm-long ribbon into bow and sew on.

2cm

2cm

How to sew on lace edging:

Follow instructions for Cover at left about sewing lace along center opening and seam.

(a) Sew side and border pieces together with gathered lace in between.

Side (Right side)

2 cm 2cm

1cm

Machine-stitch.

Border (Right side) Lace edging (Wrong side)

Gather 34cm-long lace edging

Seam allowance

Press iron-on interfacing on wrong side.

Side (Right side)

0.5cm Fold.

Lace edging (Right side)

Top-stitch.

How to make pocket:

Opening 0.2 cm 1.1cm

1cm

0.5cm

Iron-on interfacing

(Right side)

Seam allowance

Top-stitch twice along top and each side.

Seam allowance

Lace edging

0.5cm

Pocket

8cm

Machine-stitch.

0.8 cm

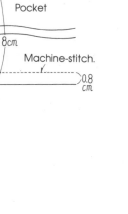

Patchwork Pictures, *shown on page 21.*

For Tulip Picture:

MATERIALS:

Sheeting: Corn yellow, 47cm by 24cm; light purple, 14cm square; old rose, 7cm square; scrap of sage green. Cotton broadcloth: Green with flowers, 16cm by 8cm; off-white with flowers, 10cm square and scrap of pink with flowers. Purple sewing thread, #50. Polyester fiberfill. Frame, 20cm in inner diameter.

FINISHED SIZE: Same size as frame.

DIRECTIONS:

①Apply glue lightly to flower and leaves, place them on piece (a) and zigzag-stitch along leaves.

②Place piece (b) on (c) and piece (a) on (b) with padding, and zigzag-stitch along piece (a).

③Pad pieces (b) and zigzag-stitch.

④Place piece (c) on (e) and zigzag-stitch.

⑤Place piece (d) as shown and zigzag-stitch along diagonal side.

⑥Pad tulip and zigzag-stitch.

⑦Place piece (e) on lining and machine-stitch 0.3cm in from edge.

⑧Pad piece (d) and zigzag-stitch along remaining two sides.

⑨Zigzag-stitch for stem and along outline of piece (e). Mount and frame.

Pattern (Actual Size)

Pink with flowers

Sage green

Diagram

Zigzag-stitch.

0.4 cm

8

8

23.5

e

d

b

c

a

Work zigzag-stitch with 0.3cm width unless otherwise indicated.

a	Old rose	7 cm square Cut 1.
b	Off-white with flowers	10 cm square Cut 1.
c	Light purple	14 cm square Cut 1.
d	Green with flowers	See diagram Cut 4.
e	Corn yellow	23.5 cm diameter Cut 1.
Lining	Corn yellow	23.5 cm diameter Cut 1.

For Square Picture:

MATERIALS:

Sheeting: Pink, sage green, dull mauve, old rose, and sky blue, 14cm by 7cm each; corn yellow, cream, sand beige, light purple, blue gray, lavender, 7cm square each. Checked cotton fabric, 12cm square. Fabric for lining and backing, 25cm square each. Sewing thread in red and purple, #50. Polyester fiberfill. Frame, 22cm square (inside measurements).

FINISHED SIZE: Same size as frame.

DIRECTIONS:

① Cut out pieces adding 0.5cm all around to each square for seam allowance but add no allowance to appliqué pieces.

② Appliqué onto square in zigzag stitch with 0.2cm width. Sew 16 pieces together following diagram.

③ Place fiberfill thinly on backing and place pieced top on fiberfill. Machine-stitch all around.

④ Zigzag-stitch with 0.2cm width along seams of motifs.

⑤ Place pieced top on lining and zigzag-stitch with 0.2cm width on each empty motif.

⑥ Zigzag-stitch with 0.5cm width all around. Mount and frame.

Diagram

Add 0.5cm all around to each motif for seam allowance.

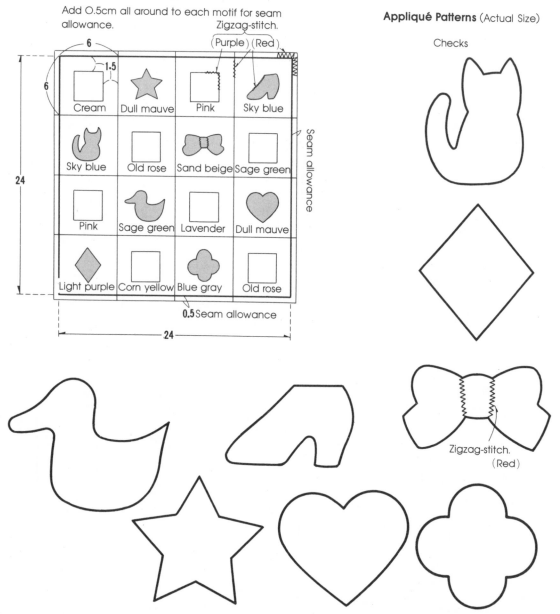

Zigzag-stitch. (Purple) (Red)

6 · 1.5 · 6 · 24 · 24

Cream	Dull mauve	Pink	Sky blue
Sky blue	Old rose	Sand beige	Sage green
Pink	Sage green	Lavender	Dull mauve
Light purple	Corn yellow	Blue gray	Old rose

Seam allowance

0.5 Seam allowance

Appliqué Patterns (Actual Size)

Checks

Zigzag-stitch. (Red)

MATERIALS:

For Boy: Off-white cotton jersey, 50cm by 15cm. Cotton broadcloth: Sky blue, 60cm by 18cm and scrap of white. Small amount of looped yarn in golden brown (same thickness as 3-ply yarn). Yellow vinyl leather, 10cm by 5cm. Yellow satin ribbon, 0.4cm by 25cm. One white semicircular button, 1cm in diameter. 2 black beads, 0.6cm in diameter. 2 gold star-shaped spangles. Elastic tape, 0.3cm by 18cm. Polyester fiberfill. Rouge. Black felt-tipped pen. For Girl: Ivory cotton jersey, 50cm by 15cm. Pink cotton broadcloth with flowers, 60cm by 18cm. Small amount of white mohair yarn (same thickness as baby yarn). White cotton lace edging, 1.8cm by 130cm. 2 black semicircular buttons, 1cm in diameter. One gold semicircular button, 0.8cm in diameter. Coral red satin ribbon, 0.8cm by 28cm. Elastic tape, 0.3cm by 18cm. Polyester fiberfill. Rouge. Black felt-tipped pen.

FINISHED SIZE: See diagrams.

Patterns (Actual Size)   Add 0.5cm for seam allowance unless otherwise indicated. Trim to 0.3cm from seam after stitching.

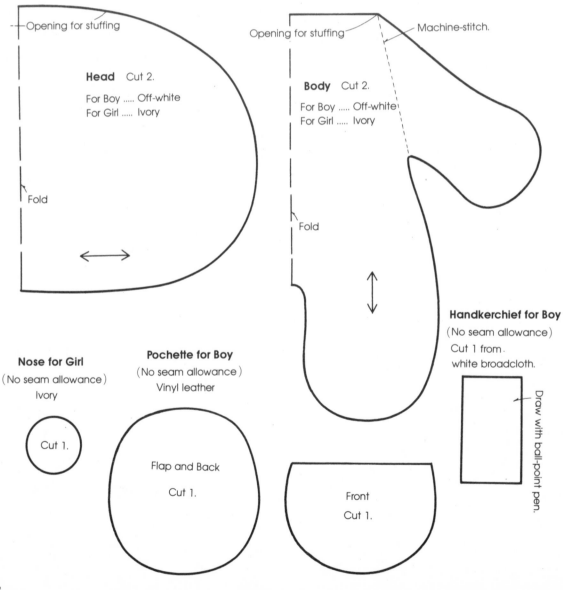

Opening for stuffing

Head   Cut 2.

For Boy ..... Off-white
For Girl ..... Ivory

Fold

Opening for stuffing   Machine-stitch.

Body   Cut 2.

For Boy ..... Off-white
For Girl ..... Ivory

Fold

Handkerchief for Boy
(No seam allowance)
Cut 1 from.
white broadcloth.

Draw with ball-point pen.

Nose for Girl
(No seam allowance)
Ivory

Cut 1.

Pochette for Boy
(No seam allowance)
Vinyl leather

Flap and Back

Cut 1.

Front
Cut 1.

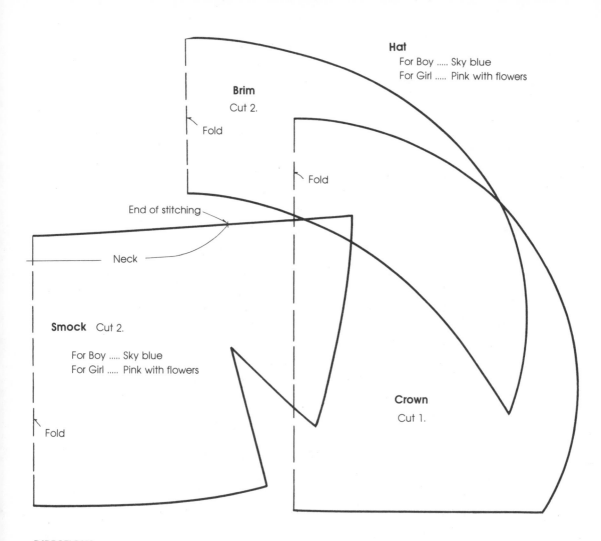

Hat
For Boy ..... Sky blue
For Girl ..... Pink with flowers

Brim
Cut 2.

Fold

Fold

End of stitching

Neck

Smock Cut 2.

For Boy ..... Sky blue
For Girl ..... Pink with flowers

Fold

Crown
Cut 1.

DIRECTIONS:

① Cut out pieces adding seam allowance.
   Note that the grain of head differs from that of body.
② With right sides facing, sew pieces for head
   together.
   Turn to right side and stuff with fiberfill.
   Make body in same manner.

③ Attach eyes (beads for Boy and buttons for Girl).
   Pull thread tightly to make hollow around eyes.

④ Sew head onto body.

Slip-stitch
opening closed.

Run gathering stitches
and pull thread
after stuffing.

Fiberfill

Stuff arms with
fiberfill and
machine-stitch.

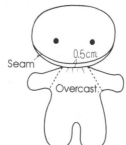

Seam

0.5cm

Overcast.

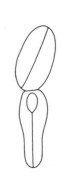

⑤ Hair

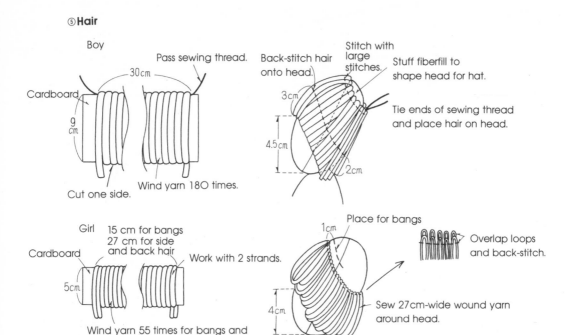

Boy

Pass sewing thread.

30cm

Cardboard

9 cm

Cut one side.

Wind yarn 180 times.

Back-stitch hair onto head.

Stitch with large stitches.

Stuff fiberfill to shape head for hat.

3cm

4.5cm

2cm

Tie ends of sewing thread and place hair on head.

Girl

15 cm for bangs
27 cm for side and back hair

Cardboard

5cm

Work with 2 strands.

Wind yarn 55 times for bangs and 100 times for side and back hair.

Place for bangs

1cm

4cm

Overlap loops and back-stitch.

Sew 27cm-wide wound yarn around head.

⑥ Hat

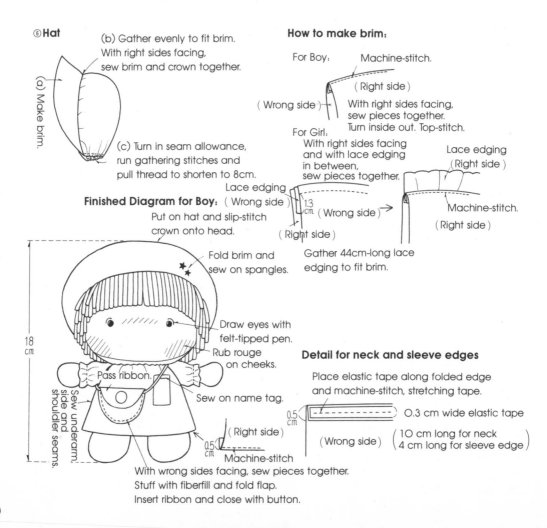

(a) Make brim.

(b) Gather evenly to fit brim. With right sides facing, sew brim and crown together.

(c) Turn in seam allowance, run gathering stitches and pull thread to shorten to 8cm.

How to make brim:

For Boy: Machine-stitch.

(Right side)

(Wrong side)

With right sides facing, sew pieces together. Turn inside out. Top-stitch.

For Girl: With right sides facing and with lace edging in between, sew pieces together.

Lace edging (Wrong side)

1.3 cm (Wrong side)

(Right side)

Lace edging (Right side)

Machine-stitch. (Right side)

Gather 44cm-long lace edging to fit brim.

Finished Diagram for Boy:

Put on hat and slip-stitch crown onto head.

Fold brim and sew on spangles.

Draw eyes with felt-tipped pen.

Rub rouge on cheeks.

Pass ribbon.

Sew on name tag.

18 cm

Sew underarm, side and shoulder seams.

(Right side)

0.5 cm

Machine-stitch

With wrong sides facing, sew pieces together.
Stuff with fiberfill and fold flap.
Insert ribbon and close with button.

Detail for neck and sleeve edges

Place elastic tape along folded edge and machine-stitch, stretching tape.

0.5 cm

0.3 cm wide elastic tape

(Wrong side)

(10 cm long for neck
4 cm long for sleeve edge)

Finished Diagram for Girl:

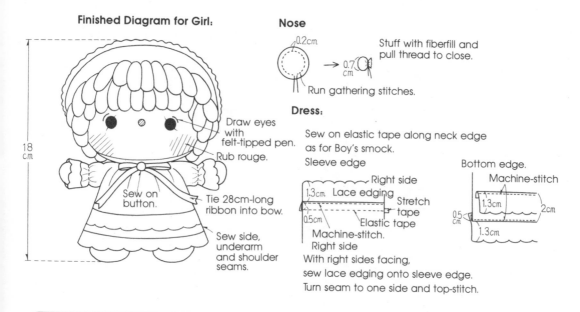

18 cm

Draw eyes with felt-tipped pen.
Rub rouge.

Sew on button.

Tie 28cm-long ribbon into bow.

Sew side, underarm and shoulder seams.

Nose

0.2cm

→ 0.7 cm

Run gathering stitches.

Stuff with fiberfill and pull thread to close.

Dress:

Sew on elastic tape along neck edge as for Boy's smock.

Sleeve edge

Right side

1.3cm Lace edging

Stretch tape

0.5cm

Elastic tape

Machine-stitch.

Right side

With right sides facing, sew lace edging onto sleeve edge. Turn seam to one side and top-stitch.

Bottom edge.

Machine-stitch

1.3cm 2cm

0.5 cm

1.3cm

Continued from page 59.

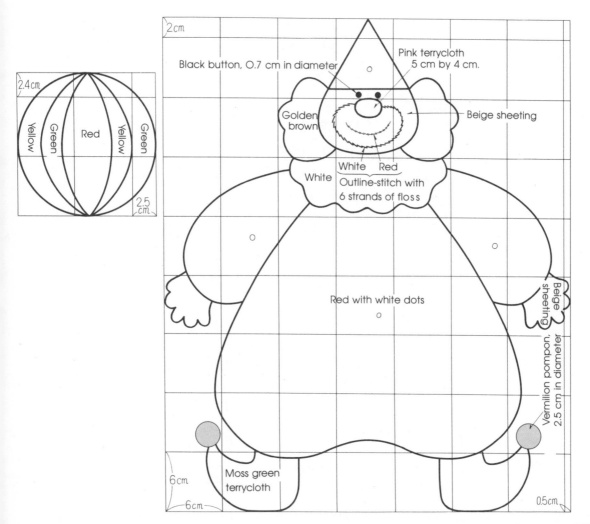

2cm

Black button, 0.7 cm in diameter

Pink terrycloth 5 cm by 4 cm.

Golden brown

Beige sheeting

White   Red

White

Outline-stitch with 6 strands of floss

Red with white dots

Beige sheeting

Vermilion pompon, 2.5 cm in diameter

6cm

Moss green terrycloth

6cm

0.5cm

2.4cm

Yellow Green Red Yellow Green

2.5 cm

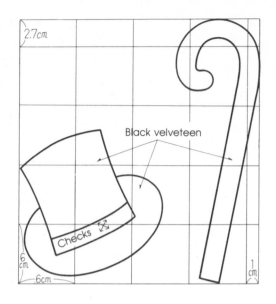

2.7cm

Black velveteen

Checks

6 cm

6cm

1 cm

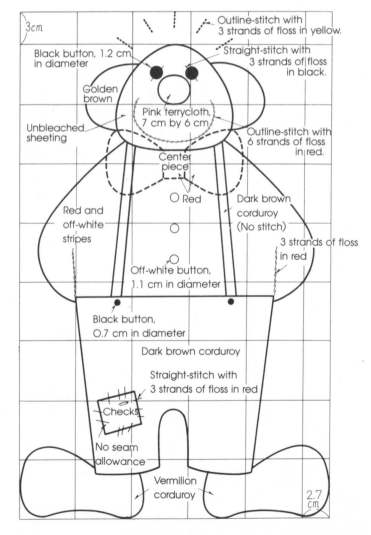

3cm

Outline-stitch with
3 strands of floss in yellow.

Black button, 1.2 cm
in diameter

Straight-stitch with
3 strands of floss
in black.

Golden
brown

Pink terrycloth,
7 cm by 6 cm

Unbleached
sheeting

Outline-stitch with
6 strands of floss
in red.

Center
piece

O Red

Dark brown
corduroy
(No stitch)

Red and
off-white
stripes

3 strands of floss
in red

O

Off-white button,
1.1 cm in diameter

Black button,
0.7 cm in diameter

Dark brown corduroy

Straight-stitch with
3 strands of floss in red

Checks

No seam
allowance

Vermilion
corduroy

2.7
cm

Pochettes, *shown on page 65.*

MATERIALS FOR ONE:

Cotton broadcloth: Spring green (cream with flowers), 82cm by 24cm; yellow (orange), 55cm square; green, 14cm by 5cm. Fabric for lining, 34cm by 25cm. Six-strand embroidery floss No. 25 in colors matching the appliqué pieces. Iron-on interfacing, 34cm by 25cm.

FINISHED SIZE: See diagram.

DIRECTIONS:

①Cut out pieces. Sew flap onto back piece in slip stitch as shown. Appliqué onto front. Sew top edges of front and lining pieces together. Press iron-on interfacing on wrong side of back and front.

②Place lining on wrong side of back piece and baste. Place lined front on lined back and bind edges with bias-cut strip. Sew shoulder strap and sew in place.

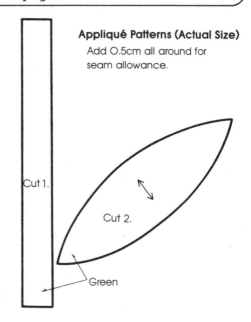

Appliqué Patterns (Actual Size)

Add 0.5cm all around for seam allowance.

Cut 1.

Cut 2.

Green

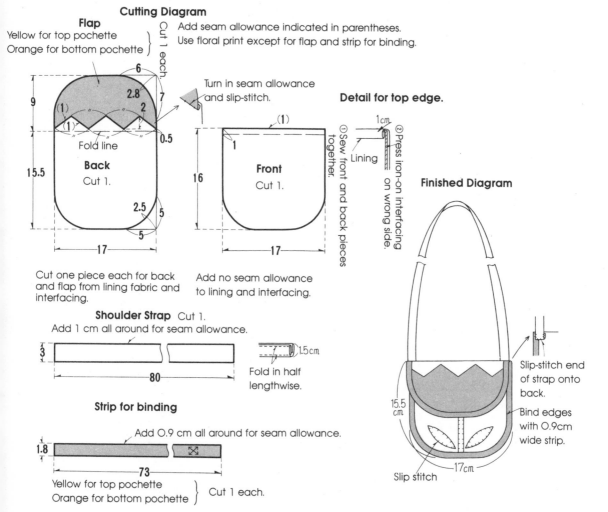

Cutting Diagram

Add seam allowance indicated in parentheses.
Use floral print except for flap and strip for binding.

Flap
Yellow for top pochette
Orange for bottom pochette
Cut 1 each.

Turn in seam allowance and slip-stitch.

Detail for top edge.

①Sew front and back pieces together.
Lining
②Press iron-on interfacing on wrong side.

Back Cut 1.

Fold line

Front Cut 1.

Cut one piece each for back and flap from lining fabric and interfacing.

Add no seam allowance to lining and interfacing.

Finished Diagram

Slip-stitch end of strap onto back.

Bind edges with 0.9cm wide strip.

Slip stitch

Shoulder Strap Cut 1.

Add 1 cm all around for seam allowance.

Fold in half lengthwise.

Strip for binding

Add 0.9 cm all around for seam allowance.

Yellow for top pochette
Orange for bottom pochette
Cut 1 each.

113

Tote Bags, *shown on page 65.*

MATERIALS:

For Pink Bag: Sheeting: Light pink, 77cm by 39cm; dark pink, 39cm by 22cm. Cotton fabric for lining, 74cm by 39cm. Cotton broadcloth: Gray, 17cm by 10cm; scraps of yellow, light pink, red with white dots, and blue with design. Six-strand embroidery floss No. 25 in red, black and colors matching the appliqué pieces. For Brown Bag: Sheeting: Gray brown, 77cm by 39cm; dark brown, 39cm by 22cm. Cotton fabric for lining, 74cm by 39cm. Cotton broadcloth: Gray, 17cm by 10cm; scraps of sky blue with leaf design, light pink, and pink with design. Gingham checks, 5cm by 8cm. Six-strand embroidery floss No. 25 in blue, red, black, and colors matching the appliqués and cotton broadcloth. For each: Iron-on interfacing, 90cm by 40cm.

FINISHED SIZE: 36cm wide and 27cm deep.

DIRECTIONS:

① Cut out pieces adding seam allowance indicated in parentheses.

② Appliqué onto pocket and embroider.

③ Press iron-on interfacing on wrong side of top and pocket.

④ Slip-stitch lining of pocket onto wrong side of appliquéd pocket along top edge as shown. Place lined pocket on bag and machine-stitch.

⑤ With right sides facing, sew side seams of outer bag and lining individually. Turn to right side.

⑥ Make handles. Sew on handles. Insert lining into outer bag and slip-stitch lining along top edge.

Cutting Diagram

Add seam allowance indicated in parentheses.

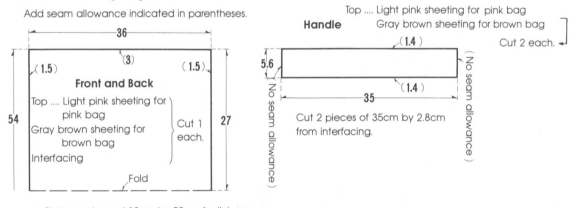

★ Cut one piece of 39cm by 55cm for lining from cotton fabric.

★ Cut one piece of 39cm by 19 cm for lining from cotton fabric.

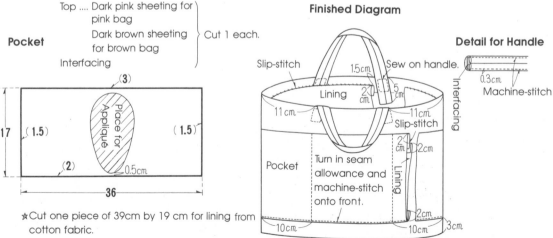

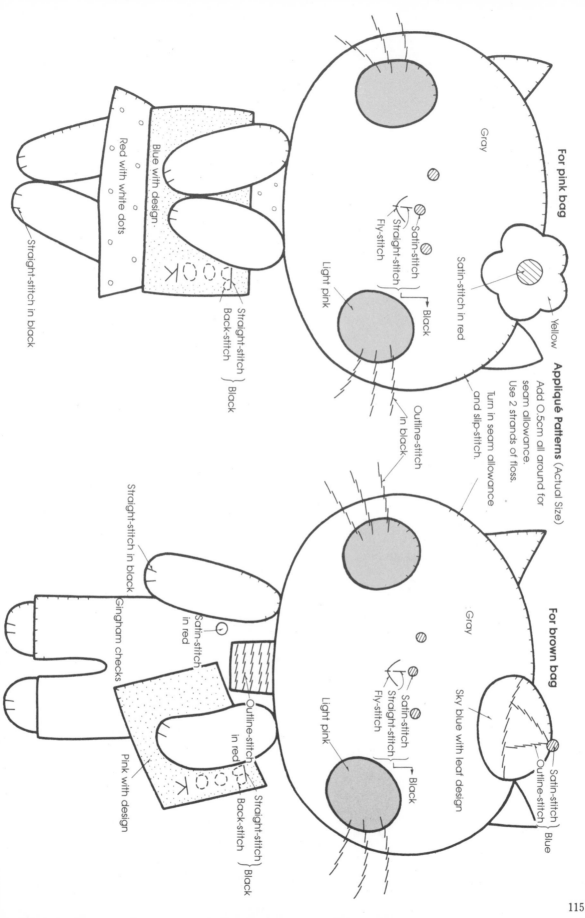

For pink bag

Gray

Red with white dots

Blue with design·

Straight-stitch in black

Straight-stitch ⎫
Back-stitch ⎭ Black

BOOK

Satin-stitch
Straight-stitch
Fly-stitch

Satin-stitch in red

→ Black

Light pink

Outline-stitch
in black

Appliqué Patterns (Actual Size)
Add 0.5cm all around for
seam allowance.
Use 2 strands of floss.
Turn in seam allowance
and slip-stitch.

Yellow

For brown bag

Gray

Straight-stitch in black

Gingham checks

Pink with design

Satin-stitch
in red

Outline-stitch
in red

Straight-stitch ⎫
Back-stitch ⎭ Black

BOOK

Satin-stitch
Straight-stitch
Fly-stitch

→ Black

Light pink

Sky blue with leaf design

Satin-stitch ⎫
Outline-stitch ⎭ Blue

115

Basic Embroidery Stitches

Satin Stitch

Outline Stitch
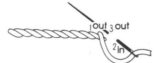

Chain Stitch

Lazy Daisy Stitch
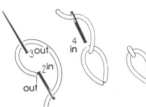

Back Stitch
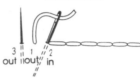

French Knot
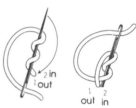

Fly Stitch
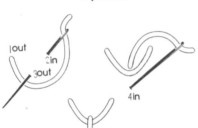

Running Stitch

Fern Stitch
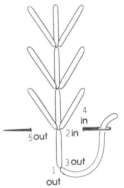

Straight Stitch

Double Cross Stitch
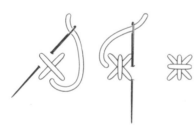

Couching

Seed Filling Stitch
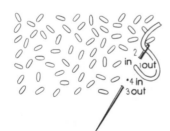

Open Buttonhole Stitch
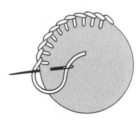

Enlarging:

Make a tracing of original design. Then draw straight lines horizontally and vertically, so that lines are equally spaced in both directions. Use second paper with larger sections and number sections in same manner. Copy design from smaller squares.

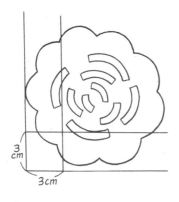

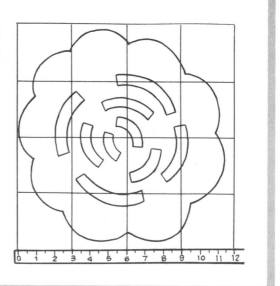

Binding:

① Place strip for binding on fabric with right sides facing. Stitch along edges.

Stitch.

Strip for binding

Right side

(By machine)

Strip for binding

Machine-stitch in the ditch.

② Turn strip over the raw edges and turn in seam allowance. Machine-stitch in the ditch.

Wrong side

(By hand)

Strip for binding

Wrong side

Turn strip over the raw edges and turn in seam allowance.

How to bind corner:

Slip-stitch.

(Wrong side)

Quilting:

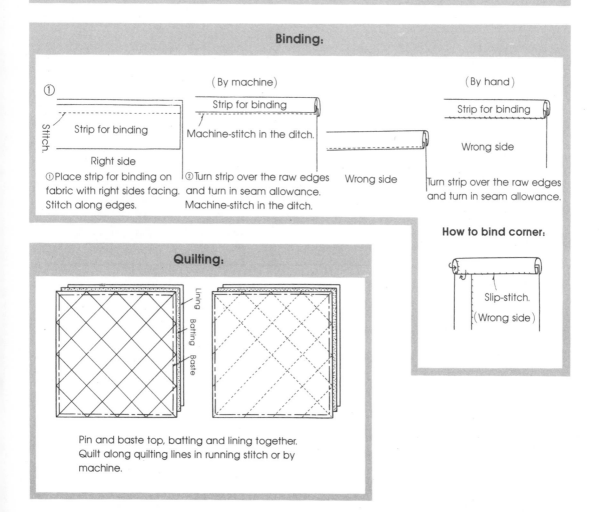

Lining

Batting

Baste

Pin and baste top, batting and lining together. Quilt along quilting lines in running stitch or by machine.

How to finish raw edges:

Zigzag-stitch.

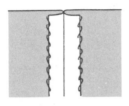

Trim off excess.

Stitch along raw edges and trim off excess.

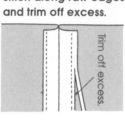

Trim off excess.

Fold raw edges and stitch.

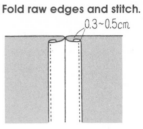

0.3~0.5cm

Overcast edges by hand.

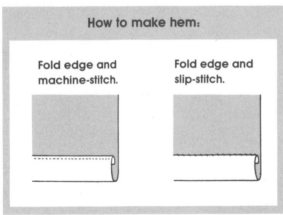

How to make hem:

Fold edge and machine-stitch.

Fold edge and slip-stitch.

Slip stitch:

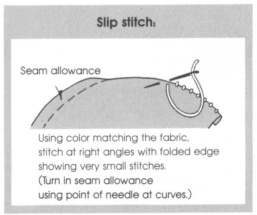

Seam allowance

Using color matching the fabric, stitch at right angles with folded edge showing very small stitches. (Turn in seam allowance using point of needle at curves.)

How to make bias tape:

Cutting

Grain line

Sewing together

Right side

Wrong side

Press seames open.

Wrong side

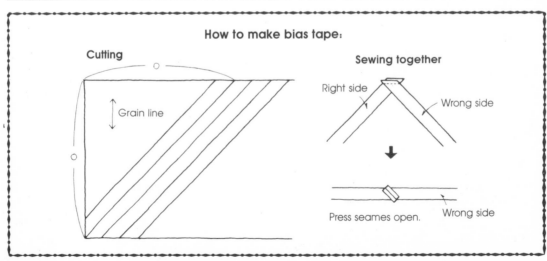